THE LEGACY OF SOVEREIGN JOY

OTHER BOOKS BY THE AUTHOR

The Justification of God:
An Exegetical and Theological Study of Romans 9:1–23
2nd Edition (Baker Book House, 1993, orig. 1983)

The Supremacy of God in Preaching
(Baker Book House, 1990)

The Pleasures of God: Meditations on God's Delight in Being God
(Multnomah Press, 1991)

Recovering Biblical Manhood and Womanhood:
A Response to Evangelical Feminism
(edited with Wayne Grudem, Crossway Books, 1991)

What's the Difference?
Manhood and Womanhood Defined According to the Bible
(Crossway Books, 1991)

Let the Nations Be Glad: The Supremacy of God in Missions
(Baker Book House, 1993)

The Purifying Power of Living by Faith in Future Grace
(Multnomah Press, 1995)

Desiring God: Meditations of a Christian Hedonist
(Multnomah Press, revised 1996)

A Hunger for God: Desiring God through Fasting and Prayer
(Crossway Books, 1997)

A Godward Life: Savoring the Supremacy of God in All of Life
(Multnomah Press, 1997)

God's Passion for His Glory: Living the Vision of Jonathan Edwards
(Crossway Books, 1998)

The Innkeeper
(Crossway Books, 1998)

A Godward Life, Book Two:
Savoring the Supremacy of God in All of Life
(Multnomah Press, 1999)

the swans are not silent

BOOK ONE

THE
Legacy of
Sovereign
Joy

God's Triumphant Grace in the Lives of
Augustine, Luther, and Calvin

JOHN PIPER

CROSSWAY BOOKS • WHEATON, ILLINOIS
A DIVISION OF GOOD NEWS PUBLISHERS

The Legacy of Sovereign Joy

Copyright © 2000 by John Piper

Published by Crossway Books
        A division of Good News Publishers
        1300 Crescent Street
        Wheaton, Illinois 60187

Cover Design: Liita Forsyth

Cover Photo: Photonica, Photographed by Daryl Solomon

Back Cover Photos: North Wind Picture Archives

Unless otherwise indicated, Bible quotations are taken from *The New American Standard Bible,* updated edition (1995), copyright © 1960, 1962, 1963, 1968, 1971, 1972, 1975, 1977, 1995 by The Lockman Foundation, and are used by permission.

First printing, 2000

Printed in the United States of America

Library of Congress Cataloging-in-Publication Data
Piper, John, 1946-
  The Legacy of Sovereign Joy: God's Triumphant Grace in the Lives of
Augustine, Luther, and Calvin / John Piper.
    p.   cm.
  Includes bibliographical references and indexes.
  ISBN 1-58134-173-3 (alk. paper)
  1. Augustine, Saint, Bishop of Hippo. 2. Luther, Martin, 1483-1546.
3. Calvin, Jean, 1509-1564. I. Title.
BR1700.2.P56 2000
270'.092'2—dc21   00-020679
[B]   CIP

| 15 | 14 | 13 | 12 | 11 | 10 | 09 | 08 | 07 | 06 | 05 | 04 | 03 | 02 |
| 15 | 14 | 13 | 12 | 11 | 10 | 9 | 8 | 7 | 6 | 5 | 4 | | |

To Jon Bloom

whose heart and hands
sustain the song
at the Bethlehem Conference For Pastors
and Desiring God Ministries

CONTENTS

The sum of all our goods,

and our perfect good,

is God.

We must not fall short of this,

nor seek anything beyond it;

the first is dangerous,

the other impossible.

ST. AUGUSTINE

MORALS OF THE CATHOLIC CHURCH, VIII, 13

PREFACE

At the age of seventy-one, four years before he died on August 28, A.D. 430, Aurelius Augustine handed over the administrative duties of the church in Hippo on the northern coast of Africa to his assistant Eraclius. Already, in his own lifetime, Augustine was a giant in the Christian world. At the ceremony, Eraclius stood to preach, as the aged Augustine sat on his bishop's throne behind him. Overwhelmed by a sense of inadequacy in Augustine's presence, Eraclius said, "The cricket chirps, the swan is silent."[1]

If only Eraclius could have looked down over sixteen centuries at the enormous influence of Augustine, he would have understood why the series of books beginning with *The Legacy of Sovereign Joy* is titled *The Swans Are Not Silent*. For 1,600 years Augustine has not been silent. In the 1500s his voice rose to a compelling crescendo in the ears of Martin Luther and John Calvin. Luther was an Augustinian monk, and Calvin quoted Augustine more than any other church father. Augustine's influence on the Protestant Reformation was extraordinary. A thousand years could not silence his song of jubilant grace. More than one historian has said, "The Reformation witnessed the ultimate triumph of Augustine's doctrine of grace over the legacy of the Pelagian view of man"[2]—the view that man is able to triumph over his own bondage to sin.

---

[1] Peter Brown, *Augustine of Hippo* (Berkeley, CA: University of California Press, 1969), p. 408.
[2] R. C. Sproul, "Augustine and Pelagius," in *Tabletalk*, June 1996, p. 11. See the Introduction in this book (note 24) for a similar statement from Benjamin Warfield. See Chapter One on the meaning of Pelagianism.

The swan also sang in the voice of Martin Luther in more than one sense. All over Germany you will find swans on church steeples, and for centuries Luther has been portrayed in works of art with a swan at his feet. Why is this? The reason goes back a century before Luther. John Hus, who died in 1415, a hundred years before Luther nailed his 95 Theses on the Wittenberg door (1517), was a professor and later president of the University of Prague. He was born of peasant stock and preached in the common language instead of Latin. He translated the New Testament into Czech, and he spoke out against abuses in the Catholic Church.

"In 1412 a papal bull was issued against Hus and his followers. Anyone could kill the Czech reformer on sight, and those who gave him food or shelter would suffer the same fate. When three of Hus' followers spoke publicly against the practice of selling indulgences, they were captured and beheaded."[3] In December 1414, Hus himself was arrested and kept in prison until March 1415. He was kept in chains and brutally tortured for his views, which anticipated the Reformation by a hundred years.

On July 6, 1415, he was burned at the stake along with his books. One tradition says that in his cell just before his death, Hus wrote, "Today, you are burning a goose [the meaning of "Hus" in Czech]; however, a hundred years from now, you will be able to hear a swan sing, you will not burn it, you will have to listen to him."[4] Martin Luther boldly saw himself as a fulfillment of this prophecy and wrote in 1531, "John Hus prophesied of me when he wrote from his prison in Bohemia: They will now roast

---

[3] Erwin Weber, "Luther with the Swan," *The Lutheran Journal*, vol. 65, no. 2, 1996, p. 10.
[4] Ibid.

a goose (for Hus means a goose), but after a hundred years they will hear a swan sing; him they will have to tolerate. And so it shall continue, if it please God."[5]

And so it has continued. The great voices of grace sing on today. And I count it a great joy to listen and to echo their song in this little book and, God willing, the ones to follow.

Although these chapters on Augustine, Luther, and Calvin were originally given as biographical messages at the annual Bethlehem Conference for Pastors (which are available on audio cassette, see page 150), there is a reason why I put them together here for a wider audience including laypeople. Their combined message is profoundly relevant in this modern world at the beginning of a new millennium. R. C. Sproul is right that "We need an Augustine or a Luther to speak to us anew lest the light of God's grace be not only overshadowed but be obliterated in our time."[6] Yes, and perhaps the best that a cricket can do is to let the swans sing.

Augustine's song of grace is unlike anything you will read in almost any modern book about grace. The omnipotent power of grace, for Augustine, is the power of "sovereign joy." This alone delivered him from a lifetime of bondage to sexual appetite and philosophical pride. Discovering that beneath the vaunted powers of human will is a cauldron of desire holding us captive to irrational choices opens the way to see grace as the triumph of "sovereign joy." Oh, how we need the ancient biblical insight of Augustine to free us from the pleasant slavery that foils the fulfillment of the Great Commandment and the finishing of the Great Commission.

---

[5] Quoted in Ewald M. Plass, *What Luther Says, An Anthology*, vol. 3 (St. Louis: Concordia Publishing House, 1959), p. 1175.

[6] R. C. Sproul, "Augustine and Pelagius," in *Tabletalk*, June 1996, p. 52.

I am not sure that Martin Luther and John Calvin saw the conquering grace of "sovereign joy" as clearly as Augustine. But what they saw even more clearly was the supremacy of the Word of God over the church and the utter necessity of sacred study at the spring of truth. Luther found his way into paradise through the gate of New Testament Greek; and Calvin bequeathed to us a 500-year legacy of God-entranced preaching because his eyes were opened to see the divine majesty of the Word. My prayer in writing this book is that, once we see Augustine's vision of grace as "sovereign joy," the lessons of Luther's study will strengthen it by the Word of God, and the lessons of Calvin's preaching will spread it to the ends of the earth. This is *The Legacy of Sovereign Joy*.

Augustine "never wrote what could be called a treatise on prayer."[7] Instead, his writing flows in and out of prayer. This is because, for him, "the whole life of a good Christian is a holy desire."[8] And this desire is for God, above all things and in all things. This is the desire I write to awaken and sustain. And therefore I pray with Augustine for myself and for you, the reader,

> Turn not away your face from me, that I may find what I seek. Turn not aside in anger from your servant, lest in seeking you I run toward something else. . . . Be my helper. Leave me not, neither despise me, O God my Savior. Scorn not that a mortal should seek the Eternal.[9]

---

[7] Thomas A. Hand, *Augustine on Prayer* (New York: Catholic Book Publishing Co., 1986), p. 11.
[8] Ibid., p. 20.
[9] Ibid., p. 27.

ACKNOWLEDGMENTS

How thankful I am for a wife and children who, several weeks each year (at least), unbegrudgingly let me live in another century. This is where I go to prepare the biographical messages for the Bethlehem Conference for Pastors. All the while, Jon Bloom, the Director of Desiring God Ministries, is masterfully managing a thousand details that bring hundreds of hungry shepherds together in the dead of winter in Minneapolis. That conference, those biographies, and this book would not exist without him and the hundreds of Bethlehem volunteers who respond to his call each year.

To steal away into the Blue Ridge Mountains for a season to put this book together in its present form has been a precious gift. I owe this productive seclusion to the hospitality of the team of God's servants at the Billy Graham Training Center at The Cove. May God grant the dream of Dr. Graham to flourish from this place—that those who attend the seminars at The Cove "will leave here transformed and prepared for action—equipped to be an effective witness for Christ."

A special word of thanks to Lane Dennis of Crossway Books for his interest in these biographical studies and his willingness to make them available to a wider audience. And thanks to Carol Steinbach again for preparing the indexes.

Finally, I thank Jesus Christ for giving to the church teachers like St. Augustine, Martin Luther, and John Calvin. "He gave some . . . pastors and teachers, for the equipping of the saints for the work of service, to the building up of the body of Christ" (Ephesians 4:11-12). I am the beneficiary of this great work of equipping the saints that these three have done for centuries. Thank you, Father, that the swans are not silent. May their song of triumphant grace continue to be sung in *The Legacy of Sovereign Joy.*

This will be written for the generation to come;

That a people yet to be created may praise the LORD.

PSALM 102:18

One generation shall praise Your works to another,

And shall declare Your mighty acts.

PSALM 145:4

Savoring the Sovereignty of Grace

in the Lives of Flawed Saints

The Point of History

God ordains that we gaze on his glory, dimly mirrored in the ministry of his flawed servants. He intends for us to consider their lives and peer through the imperfections of their faith and behold the beauty of their God. "Remember your leaders, those who spoke to you the word of God; consider the outcome of their life, and imitate their faith" (Hebrews 13:7, RSV). The God who fashions the hearts of all men (Psalm 33:15) means for their lives to display his truth and his worth. From Phoebe to St. Francis, the divine plan—even spoken of the pagan Pharaoh—holds firm for all: "I have raised you up for the very purpose of showing my power in you, so that my name may be proclaimed in all the earth" (Romans 9:17, RSV). From David, the king, to David Brainerd, the missionary, extraordinary and incomplete specimens of godliness and wisdom have kindled the worship of sovereign grace in the hearts of reminiscing saints. "This will be written for the generation to come, that a people yet to be created may praise the LORD" (Psalm 102:18).

The history of the world is a field strewn with broken stones, which are sacred altars designed to waken worship in the hearts of those who will take the time to read and remember. "I shall remember the deeds of the LORD; surely I will remember Your wonders of old. I will meditate on all Your work and muse on Your deeds. Your way, O God, is holy; what god is great like our God?" (Psalm 77:11-13). The aim of providence in the history of the world is the worship of the people of God. Ten thousand stories of grace and truth are meant to be remembered for the refinement of faith and the sustaining of hope and the guidance of love. "Whatever was written in former days was written for our instruction, that by steadfastness and by the encouragement of the scriptures we might have hope" (Romans 15:4, RSV). Those who nurture their hope in the history of grace will live their lives to the glory of God. That is the aim of this book.

It is a book about three famous and flawed fathers in the Christian church. Therefore, it is a book about grace, not only because the faithfulness of God triumphs over the flaws of men, but also because this was the very theme of their lives and work. Aurelius Augustine (354-430), Martin Luther (1483-1546), and John Calvin (1509-1564) had this in common: they experienced, and then built their lives and ministries on, the reality of God's omnipotent grace. In this way their common passion for the supremacy of God was preserved from the taint of human competition. Each of them confessed openly that the essence of experiential Christianity is the glorious triumph of grace over the guilty impotence of man.

Augustine's Discovery of "Sovereign Joy"

At first Augustine resisted the triumph of grace as an enemy. But then, in a garden in Milan, Italy, when he was thirty-one, the power of grace through the truth of God's Word broke fifteen years of bondage to sexual lust and living with a concubine. His resistance was finally overcome by "sovereign joy," the beautiful name he gave to God's grace. "How sweet all at once it was for me to be rid of those fruitless joys which I had once feared to lose . . . ! You drove them from me, you who are the true, the *sovereign joy*. You drove them from me and took their place, you who are sweeter than all pleasure. . . . O Lord my God, my Light, my Wealth, and my Salvation."[1]

Then, in his maturity, and to the day of his death, Augustine fought the battle for grace as a submissive captive to "sovereign joy" against his contemporary and arch-antagonist, the British monk, Pelagius. Nothing shocked Pelagius more than the stark declaration of omnipotent grace in Augustine's prayer, "Command what you wish, but give what you command."[2] Augustine knew that his liberty from lust and his power to live for Christ and his understanding of biblical truth hung on the validity of that prayer. He was painfully aware of the hopelessness of leaning on free will as a help against lust.

> Who is not aghast at the sudden crevasses that might open in the life of a dedicated man? When I was writing this, we were told that a man of 84, who had lived a life of continence under religious observance with a pious wife for 25 years, has gone and bought himself a music-girl for his pleasure. . . . If the angels were left to their own free-will, even they might lapse, and the world be filled with "new devils."[3]

---

[1] Aurelius Augustine, *Confessions*, trans. R. S. Pine-Coffin (New York: Penguin Books, 1961), p. 181 (IX, 1), italics added.

[2] Peter Brown, *Augustine of Hippo* (Berkeley, CA: University of California Press, 1969), p. 179. The quote is found in Augustine, *Confessions*, X, xxix, p. 40.

[3] Peter Brown, *Augustine of Hippo*, p. 405, quoting *Contra Julian*, III, x, 22.

Augustine knew that the same would happen to him if God left
him to lean on his own free will for faith and purity. The battle
for omnipotent grace was not theoretical or academic; it was practical and pressing. At stake was holiness and heaven. Therefore
he fought with all his might for the supremacy of grace against
the Pelagian exaltation of man's ultimate self-determination.[4]

Luther's Pathway into Paradise

For Martin Luther, the triumph of grace came not in a garden
but in a study, and not primarily over lust but over the fear of
God's wrath. "If I could believe that God was not angry with
me, I would stand on my head for joy."[5] He might have said, "sovereign joy." But he could not believe it. And the great external
obstacle was not a concubine in Milan, Italy, but a biblical text
in Wittenberg, Germany. "A single word in [Romans 1:17], 'In
[the gospel] the *righteousness of God* is revealed' . . . stood in my
way. For I hated that word 'righteousness of God.'"[6] He had been
taught that the "righteousness of God" meant the justice "with
which God is righteous and punishes the unrighteous sinner."[7]
This was no relief and no gospel. Whereas Augustine "tore [his]
hair and hammered [his] forehead with his fists" in hopelessness
over bondage to sexual passion,[8] Luther "raged with a fierce and

[4] The book Augustine himself saw as his "most fundamental demolition of Pelagianism"
(Peter Brown, *Augustine of Hippo*, p. 372) is entitled *On the Spirit and the Letter*, in *Augustine:
Later Works*, ed. John Burnaby (Philadelphia: Westminster Press, 1965), pp. 182-251.
[5] Heiko A. Oberman, *Luther: Man Between God and the Devil*, trans. Eileen Walliser-
Schwarzbart (New York: Doubleday, 1992, orig. 1982), p. 315.
[6] John Dillenberger, ed., *Martin Luther: Selections from His Writings* (Garden City, NY:
Doubleday and Co., 1961), p. 11, emphasis added.
[7] Ibid.
[8] "I was beside myself with madness that would bring me sanity. I was dying a death that would
bring me life. . . . I was frantic, overcome by violent anger with myself for not accepting your will
and entering into your covenant. . . . I tore my hair and hammered my forehead with my fists; I
locked my fingers and hugged my knees," Augustine, *Confessions*, pp. 170-171 (VIII, 8).

troubled conscience . . . [and] beat importunately upon Paul at that place [Romans 1:17], most ardently desiring to know what St. Paul wanted."[9]

The breakthrough came in 1518, not, as with Augustine, by the sudden song of a child chanting, "Take it and read,"[10] but by the unrelenting study of the historical-grammatical context of Romans 1:17. This sacred study proved to be a precious means of grace. "At last, by the mercy of God, meditating day and night, I gave heed to the context of the words, namely . . . 'He who through faith is righteous shall live.' There I began to understand [that] the righteousness of God is that by which the righteous lives by a gift of God, namely by faith. . . . Here I felt that I was altogether born again and had entered paradise itself through open gates."[11] This was the joy that turned the world upside-down.

Justification by faith alone, apart from works of the law, was the triumph of grace in the life of Martin Luther. He did, you might say, stand on his head for joy, and with him all the world was turned upside-down. But the longer he lived, the more he was convinced that there was a deeper issue beneath this doctrine and its conflict with the meritorious features of indulgences[12] and purgatory. In the end, it was not Johann Tetzel's sale of indulgences or Johann Eck's promotion of purgatory that produced Luther's most passionate defense of God's omnipotent grace; it was Desiderius Erasmus' defense of free will.

Erasmus was to Luther what Pelagius was to Augustine. Martin Luther conceded that Erasmus, more than any other oppo-

---

[9] Dillenberger, ed., *Martin Luther: Selections from His Writings*, p. 12.
[10] See Chapter One of this book for the details of this remarkable story.
[11] Dillenberger, ed., *Martin Luther: Selections from His Writings*, p. 12.
[12] Indulgences were the sale of release from temporal punishment for sin through the payment of money to the Roman Catholic Church—for yourself or another in purgatory.

nent, had realized that the powerlessness of man before God, not the indulgence controversy or purgatory, was the central question of the Christian faith.[13] Luther's book *The Bondage of the Will*, published in 1525, was an answer to Erasmus' book *The Freedom of the Will*. Luther regarded this one book of his—*The Bondage of the Will*—as his "best theological book, and the only one in that class worthy of publication."[14] This is because at the heart of Luther's theology was a total dependence on the freedom of God's omnipotent grace to rescue powerless man from the bondage of the will. "Man cannot by his own power purify his heart and bring forth godly gifts, such as true repentance for sins, a true, as over against an artificial, fear of God, true faith, sincere love. . . ."[15] Erasmus' exaltation of man's fallen will as free to overcome its own sin and bondage was, in Luther's mind, an assault on the freedom of God's grace and therefore an attack on the very gospel itself, and ultimately on the glory of God. Thus Luther proved himself to be a faithful student of St. Augustine and St. Paul to the very end.

Calvin's Encounter with the Divine Majesty of the Word

For John Calvin, the triumph of God's grace in his own life and theology was the self-authenticating demonstration of the majesty of God in the Word of Scripture. How are we to know that the Bible is the Word of God? Do we lean on the testimony of man—the authority of the church, as in Roman

---

[13] Oberman, *Luther: Man Between God and the Devil*, p. 220.
[14] Dillenberger, ed., *Martin Luther: Selections from His Writings*, p. 167.
[15] Conrad Bergendoff, ed., *Church and Ministry II*, vol. 40, *Luther's Works* (Philadelphia: Muhlenberg Press, 1958), p. 301.

Catholicism? Or are we more immediately dependent on the majesty of God's grace? Sometime in his early twenties, before 1533, at the University of Paris, Calvin's resistance to grace was conquered for the glory of God and for the cause of the Reformation. "God, by a sudden conversion subdued and brought my mind to a teachable frame. . . . Having thus received some taste and knowledge of true godliness, I was immediately inflamed with [an] intense desire to make progress."[16] With this "taste" and this "intense desire" the legacy of Sovereign Joy took root in another generation.

The power that "subdued" his mind was the manifestation of the majesty of God. "Our Heavenly Father, revealing *his majesty* [in Scripture], lifts reverence for Scripture beyond the realm of controversy."[17] There is the key for Calvin: the witness of God to Scripture is the immediate, unassailable, life-giving revelation to our minds of *the majesty of God* that is manifest in the Scriptures themselves. This was his testimony to the omnipotent grace of God in his life: The blind eyes of his spirit were opened, and what he saw immediately, and without a lengthy chain of human reasoning, were two things so interwoven that they would determine the rest of his life: the majesty of God and the Word of God. The Word mediated the majesty, and the majesty vindicated the Word. Henceforth he would be a man utterly devoted to displaying the supremacy of God's glory by the exposition of God's Word.

---

[16] Dillenberger, *John Calvin, Selections from His Writings*, p. 26.
[17] John Calvin, *Institutes of the Christian Religion*, in two volumes, ed. John T. McNeil, trans. Ford Lewis Battles (Philadelphia: The Westminster Press, 1960), I, viii, 13 (emphasis added).

United with a Passion for the Supremacy of Divine Grace

In all of this, Augustine, Luther, and Calvin were one. Their passion was to display above all things the glory of God through the exaltation of his omnipotent grace. Augustine's entire life was one great "confession" of the glory of God's grace: "O Lord, my Helper and my Redeemer, I shall now tell and confess *to the glory of your name* how you released me from the fetters of lust which held me so tightly shackled and from my slavery to the things of this world."[18] From the beginning of Luther's discovery of grace, displaying the glory of God was the driving force of his labor. "I recall that at the beginning of my cause Dr. Staupitz, who was then a man of great importance and vicar of the Augustinian Order, said to me: 'It pleases me that the doctrine which you preach ascribes the glory and everything to God alone and nothing to man.'"[19] Calvin's course was fixed from his first dispute with Cardinal Sadolet in 1539 when he charged the Cardinal to "set before [man], as the prime motive of his existence, *zeal to illustrate the glory of God.*"[20]

Under Christ, Augustine's influence on Luther and Calvin was second only to the influence of the apostle Paul. Augustine towers over the thousand years between himself and the Reformation, heralding the Sovereign Joy of God's triumphant grace for all generations. Adolf Harnack said that he was the greatest man "between Paul the Apostle and Luther the Reformer, the Christian Church has possessed."[21] The standard text on theology that

---

[18] Augustine, *Confessions*, p.166 (VIII, 6).

[19] Ewald M. Plass, compiler, *What Luther Says: An Anthology*, vol. 3 (St. Louis: Concordia Publishing House, 1959), p. 1374.

[20] Dillenberger, *John Calvin, Selections from His Writings*, p. 89 (emphasis added).

[21] Quoted from "Monasticism and the Confessions of St. Augustine," in Benjamin Warfield, *Calvin and Augustine* (Philadelphia: The Presbyterian and Reformed Publishing Co., 1971), p. 306. Although "his direct work as a reformer of Church life was done in a corner, and its results were immediately swept away by the flood of the Vandal invasion . . . it was through his voluminous writings, by which his wider influence was exerted, that he entered both the

Calvin and Luther drank from was *Sentences* by Peter Lombard. Nine-tenths of this book consists of quotations from Augustine, and it was for centuries *the* textbook for theological studies.[22] Luther was an Augustinian monk, and Calvin immersed himself in the writings of Augustine, as we can see from the increased use of Augustine's writings in each new edition of the *Institutes*. "In the 1536 edition of the *Institutes* he quotes Augustine 20 times, three years later 113, in 1543 it was 128 times, 141 in 1550 and finally, no less than 342 in 1559."[23]

Not surprisingly, therefore, yet paradoxically, one of the most esteemed fathers of the Roman Catholic Church "gave us the Reformation." Benjamin Warfield put it like this: "The Reformation, inwardly considered, was just the ultimate triumph of Augustine's doctrine of grace over Augustine's doctrine of the Church."[24] In other words, there were tensions within Augustine's

---

Church and the world as a revolutionary force, and not merely created an epoch in the history of the Church, but has determined the course of its history in the West up to the present day" (Warfield, *Calvin and Augustine*, p. 306). "Anselm, Aquinas, Petrarch (never without a pocket copy of the *Confessions*), Luther, Bellarmine, Pascal, and Kierkegaard all stand in the shade of his broad oak. His writings were among the favourite books of Wittgenstein. He was the *bête noire* of Nietzsche. His psychological analysis anticipated parts of Freud: he first discovered the existence of the 'sub-conscious.' . . . He was 'the first modern man' in the sense that with him the reader feels himself addressed at a level of extraordinary psychological depth and confronted by a coherent system of thought, large parts of which still make potent claims to attention and respect" (Henry Chadwick, *Augustine* [Oxford: Oxford University Press, 1986], p. 3).

[22] Trapè, Agostino, *Saint Augustine: Man, Pastor, Mystic* (New York: Catholic Book Publishing, 1986), pp. 333-334.

[23] T. H. L. Parker, *Portrait of Calvin* (Philadelphia: Westminster Press, 1954), p. 44.

[24] Warfield, *Calvin and Augustine*, pp. 322-323. "This doctrine of grace came from Augustine's hands in its positive outline completely formulated: sinful man depends, for his recovery to good and to God, entirely on the free grace of God; this grace is therefore indispensable, prevenient, irresistible, indefectible; and, being thus the free grace of God, must have lain, in all the details of its conference and working, in the intention of God from all eternity. But, however clearly announced and forcefully commended by him, it required to make its way against great obstacles in the Church. As over against the Pelagians, the indispensableness of grace was quickly established; as over against the Semi-Pelagians, its prevenience was with almost equal rapidity made good. But there advance paused. If the necessity of prevenient grace was thereafter (after the Council of Orange, 529) the established doctrine of the Church, the irresistibility of this prevenient grace was put under the ban, and there remained no place for a complete 'Augustinianism' within the Church. . . . Therefore, when the great revival of religion which we call the Reformation came, seeing that it was, on its theological side, a revival of 'Augustinianism,' as all great revivals of religion must be (for 'Augustinianism' is but the thetical expression of religion in its purity), there was nothing for it but the rending of the Church. And therefore also the greatest peril to the Reformation was and remains the diffused anti-'Augustinianism' in the world."

thought that explain why he could be cited by both Roman Catholics and by Reformers as a champion.

God's Grace over the Flaws of Great Saints

This brings us back to an earlier point. This book, which is about Augustine, Luther, and Calvin, is a book about the glory of God's omnipotent grace, not only because it was the unifying theme of their work, but also because this grace triumphed over the flaws in these men's lives. Augustine's most famous work is called the *Confessions* in large measure because his whole ministry was built on the wonder that God could forgive and use a man who had sold himself to so much sensuality for so long. And now we add to this imperfection the flaws of Augustine's theology suggested by Warfield's comment that his doctrine of grace triumphed over his doctrine of the church. Of course, this will be disputed. But from my perspective he is correct to draw attention to Augustine's weaknesses amid massive strengths.

Augustine's Dubious Record on Sex and Sacraments

For example, it is a perplexing incongruity that Augustine would exalt the free and sovereign grace of God so supremely and yet hold to a view of baptism that makes the act of man so decisive in the miracle of regeneration. Baptismal regeneration and spiritual awakening by the power of the Word of God do not fit together. The way Augustine speaks of baptism seems to go against his entire experience of God's grace, awakening and transforming him through the Word of God in Milan. In the

Confessions he mentions a friend who was baptized while unconscious and comes to his senses changed.[25] "In a way that Augustine never claimed to understand, the physical rites of baptism and ordination 'brand' a permanent mark on the recipient, quite independent of his conscious qualities."[26] He regretted not having been baptized as a youth and believed that ritual would have spared him much misery. "It would have been much better if I had been healed at once and if all that I and my family could do had been done to make sure that once my soul had received its salvation, its safety should be left in your keeping, since its salvation had come from you. This would surely have been the better course."[27] Peter Brown writes that Augustine "had once hoped to understand the rite of infant baptism: 'Reason will find that out.' Now he will appeal, not to reason, but to the rooted feelings of the Catholic masses."[28]

Of course, Augustine is not alone in mingling a deep knowledge of grace with defective views and flawed living. Every worthy theologian and every true saint does the same. Every one of them confesses, "Now we see in a mirror dimly, but then face to face; now I know in part, but then I shall know fully just as I also have been fully known" (1 Corinthians 13:12). "Not that I have already obtained it, or have already become perfect, but I press on in order that I may lay hold of that for which also I was laid hold of by Christ Jesus" (Philippians 3:12). But the famous flawed saints have their flaws exposed and are criticized vigorously for it.

---

[25] Cited in Brown, *Augustine of Hippo*, p. 222 (IV, iv, 8).
[26] Ibid., p. 222.
[27] Augustine, *Confessions*, p. 32 (I, 11).
[28] Brown, *Augustine of Hippo*, p. 280.

Diverse Defects of Different Men

Martin Luther and John Calvin were seriously flawed saints. The flaws grew in the soil of very powerful—and very different—personalities.

> How different the upbringing of the two men—the one, the son of a German miner, singing for his livelihood under the windows of the well-do-do burghers; the other, the son of a French procurator-fiscal, delicately reared and educated with the children of the nobility. How different, too, their temperaments—Luther, hearty, jovial, jocund, sociable, filling his goblet day by day from the Town Council's wine-cellar; Calvin, lean, austere, retiring, given to fasting and wakefulness. . . . Luther was a man of the people, endowed with passion, poetry, imagination, fire, whereas Calvin was cold, refined, courteous, able to speak to nobles and address crowned heads, and seldom, if ever, needing to retract or even to regret his words.[29]

Luther's Dirty Mouth and Lapse of Love

But, oh, how many words did Luther regret! This was the downside of a delightfully blunt and open emotional life, filled with humor as well as anger. Heiko Oberman refers to Luther's "jocular theologizing."[30] "If I ever have to find myself a wife again, I will hew myself an obedient wife out of stone."[31] "In domestic affairs I defer to Katie. Otherwise I am led by the Holy Ghost."[32] "I have legitimate children, which no papal theologian has."[33] His

---

[29] Henry F. Henderson, *Calvin in His Letters* (London: J. M. Dent and Co., 1909), pp. 109-110.
[30] Oberman, *Luther: Man Between God and the Devil*, p. 5.
[31] Ibid., p. 276.
[32] William J. Peterson, *Martin Luther Had a Wife* (Wheaton: Tyndale House, 1983), p. 14.
[33] Oberman, *Luther: Man Between God and the Devil*, p. 278.

personal experience is always present. "With Luther feelings force their way everywhere. . . . He himself is passionately present, not only teaching life by faith but living faith himself."[34] This makes him far more interesting and attractive as a person than Calvin, but far more volatile and offensive—depending on what side of the joke you happen to be on. We cannot imagine today (as much as we might like to) a university professor doing theology the way Luther did it. The leading authority on Luther comments, "[Luther] would look in vain for a chair in theology today at Harvard. . . . It is the Erasmian type of ivory-tower academic that has gained international acceptance."[35]

With all its spice, his language could also move toward crudity and hatefulness. His longtime friend, Melanchthon, did not hesitate to mention Luther's "sharp tongue" and "heated temper" even as he gave his funeral oration.[36] There were also the four-letter words and the foul "bathroom" talk. He confessed from time to time that it was excessive. "Many accused me of proceeding too severely. Severely, that is true, and often too severely; but it was a question of the salvation of all, even my opponents."[37]

We who are prone to fault him for his severity and mean-spirited language can scarcely imagine what the battle was like in those days, and what it was like to be the target of so many vicious, slanderous, and life-threatening attacks. "He could not say a word that would not be heard and pondered everywhere."[38] It will be fair to let Luther and one of his balanced admirers put his harshness and his crudeness in perspective. First Luther himself:

---

[34] Ibid., pp. 312-313.
[35] Ibid., p. 313.
[36] Ibid., p. 10.
[37] Ibid., p. 322.
[38] Ibid., p. 298.

I own that I am more vehement than I ought to be; but I have to do with men who blaspheme evangelical truth; with human wolves; with those who condemn me unheard, without admonishing, without instructing me; and who utter the most atrocious slanders against myself not only, but the Word of God. Even the most phlegmatic spirit, so circumstanced, might well be moved to speak thunderbolts; much more I who am choleric by nature, and possessed of a temper easily apt to exceed the bounds of moderation.

I cannot, however, but be surprised to learn whence the novel taste arose which daintily calls everything spoken against an adversary abusive and acrimonious. What think ye of Christ? Was he a reviler when he called the Jews an adulterous and perverse generation, a progeny of vipers, hypocrites, children of the devil?

What think you of Paul? Was he abusive when he termed the enemies of the gospel dogs and seducers? Paul who, in the thirteenth chapter of the Acts, inveighs against a false prophet in this manner: "Oh, full of subtlety and all malice, thou child of the devil, thou enemy of all right-eousness." I pray you, good Spalatin, read me this riddle. *A mind conscious of truth cannot always endure the obstinate and willfully blind enemies of truth.* I see that all persons demand of me moderation, and especially those of my adversaries, who least exhibit it. If I am too warm, I am at least open and frank; in which respect I excel those who always smile, but murder.[39]

It may seem futile to ponder the positive significance of filthy language, but let the reader judge whether "the world's foremost authority on Luther"[40] helps us grasp a partially redemptive purpose in Luther's occasionally foul mouth.

---

[39] W. Carlos Martyn, *The Life and Times of Martin Luther* (New York: American Tract Society, 1866), pp. 380-381.
[40] The plaudit comes from professor Steven Ozment of Harvard University printed on the back of Heiko A. Oberman, *Luther: Man Between God and the Devil.*

Luther's scatology-permeated language has to be taken seriously as an expression of the painful battle fought body and soul against the Adversary, who threatens both flesh and spirit. . . . The filthy vocabulary of Reformation propaganda aimed at inciting the common man. . . . Luther used a great deal of invective, but there was method in it. . . . Inclination and conviction unite to form a mighty alliance, fashioning a new language of filth which is more than filthy language. Precisely in all its repulsiveness and perversion it verbalizes the unspeakable: the diabolic profanation of God and man. Luther's lifelong barrage of crude words hurled at the opponents of the Gospel is robbed of significance if attributed to bad breeding. When taken seriously, it reveals the task Luther saw before him: to do battle against the greatest slanderer of all times![41]

Nevertheless most will agree that even though the thrust and breakthrough of the Reformation against such massive odds required someone of Luther's forcefulness, a line was often crossed into unwarranted invective and sin. Heiko Oberman is surely right to say, "Where resistance to the Papal State, fanaticism, and Judaism turns into the collective vilification of papists, Anabaptists, and Jews, the fatal point has been reached where the discovery of the Devil's power becomes a liability and a danger."[42] Luther's sometimes malicious anti-Semitism was an inexcusable contradiction of the Gospel he preached. Oberman observes with soberness and depth that Luther aligned himself with the Devil here, and the lesson to be learned is that this is possible for Christians, and to demythologize it is to leave Luther's anti-Semitism in the hands of modern unbelief with no weapon

---

[41] Ibid., p. 109.
[42] Ibid., p. 303.

against it.[43] In other words, the devil is real and can trip a great man into graceless behavior, even as he recovers grace from centuries of obscurity.

Calvin's Accommodation to Brutal Times

John Calvin was very different from Luther but just as much a child of his harsh and rugged age. He and Luther never met, but had profound respect for each other. When Luther read Calvin's defense of the Reformation to Cardinal Sadolet in 1539 he said, "Here is a writing which has hands and feet. I rejoice that God raises up such men."[44] Calvin returned the respect in the one letter to Luther that we know of, which Luther did not receive. "Would that I could fly to you that I might, even for a few hours, enjoy the happiness of your society; for I would prefer, and it would be far better . . . to converse personally with yourself; but seeing that it is not granted to us on earth, I hope that shortly it will come to pass in the kingdom of God."[45] Knowing their circumstances better than we, and perhaps knowing their own sins better than we, they could pass over each other's flaws more easily in their affections.

It has not been so easy for others. The greatness of the accolades for John Calvin have been matched by the seriousness and severity of the criticisms. In his own day, even his brilliant contemporaries stood in awe of Calvin's grasp of the fullness of Scripture. At the 1541 Conference at Worms, Melanchthon expressed that he was overwhelmed at Calvin's learning and called

---

[43] Ibid., p. 297.
[44] Henderson, *Calvin in His Letters*, p. 68.
[45] Ibid., pp. 113-114.

him simply "The Theologian." In modern times, T. H. L. Parker agrees and says, "Augustine and Luther were perhaps his superiors in creative thinking; Aquinas in philosophy; but in systematic theology Calvin stands supreme."[46] And Benjamin Warfield said, "No man ever had a profounder sense of God than he."[47] But the times were barbarous, and not even Calvin could escape the evidences of his own sinfulness and the blind spots of his own age.

Life was harsh, even brutal, in the sixteenth century. There was no sewer system or piped water supply or central heating or refrigeration or antibiotics or penicillin or aspirin or surgery for appendicitis or Novocain for tooth extraction or electric lights for studying at night or water heaters or washers or dryers or stoves or ballpoint pens or typewriters or computers. Calvin, like many others in his day, suffered from "almost continuous ill-health."[48] If life could be miserable physically, it could get even more dangerous socially and more grievous morally. The libertines in Calvin's church, like their counterparts in first-century Corinth, reveled in treating the "communion of saints" as a warrant for wife-swapping.[49] Calvin's opposition made him the victim of mob violence and musket fire more than once.

Not only were the times unhealthy, harsh, and immoral, they

---

[46] Parker, *Portrait of Calvin*, p. 49. Jakobus Arminius, usually considered the historic antagonist of Calvinism, wrote, "[Calvin] excels beyond comparison in the interpretation of Scripture, and his commentaries ought to be more highly valued than all that is handed down to us by the Library of the Fathers" (Alfred T. Davies, *John Calvin and the Influence of Protestantism on National Life and Character* [London: Henry E. Walter, 1946], p. 24). "He stands out in the history of biblical study as, what Diestel, for example, proclaims him, 'the creator of genuine exegesis.' The authority which his comments immediately acquired was immense—they 'opened the Scriptures' as the Scriptures never had been opened before. Richard Hooker—'the judicious Hooker'—remarks that in the controversies of his own time, 'the sense of Scripture which Calvin alloweth' was of more weight than if 'ten thousand Augustines, Jeromes, Chrysostoms, Cyprians were brought forward'" (Warfield, *Calvin and Augustine*, p. 9).

[47] Warfield, *Calvin and Augustine*, p. 24.

[48] John Calvin, *Sermons on the Epistle to the Ephesians* (Edinburgh: The Banner of Truth Trust, 1973, orig. in English 1577, orig. in French 1562), with Introduction by the publishers, p. viii. For details on Calvin's miseries see Chapter Three.

[49] Henderson, *Calvin in His Letters*, p. 75.

were often barbaric as well. This is important to see, because
Calvin did not escape the influence of his times. He described in
a letter the cruelty common in Geneva. "A conspiracy of men
and women has lately been discovered who, for the space of three
years, had [intentionally] spread the plague through the city, by
what mischievous device I know not." The upshot of this was that
fifteen women were burned at the stake. "Some men," Calvin said,
"have even been punished more severely; some have committed
suicide in prison, and while twenty-five are still kept prisoners, the
conspirators do not cease . . . to smear the door-locks of the
dwelling-houses with their poisonous ointment."[50]

This kind of capital punishment loomed on the horizon not
just for criminals, but for the Reformers themselves. Calvin was driven out of his homeland, France, under threat of death. For the next
twenty years he agonized over the martyrs there and corresponded
with many of them as they walked faithfully toward the stake. The
same fate easily could have befallen Calvin with the slightest turn
in providence. "We have not only exile to fear, but that all the most
cruel varieties of death are impending over us, for in the cause of
religion they will set no bounds to their barbarity."[51]

This atmosphere gave rise to the greatest and the worst achievement of Calvin. The greatest was the writing of the *Institutes of
the Christian Religion*, and the worst was his joining in the con-
demnation of the heretic, Michael Servetus, to burning at the stake
in Geneva. The *Institutes* was first published in March 1536, when
Calvin was twenty-six years old. It went through five editions and
enlargements until it reached its present form in the 1559 edition.

---

[50] Ibid., p. 63.
[51] Dillenberger, *John Calvin, Selections from His Writings*, p. 71.

If this were all Calvin had written—and not forty-eight volumes of other works—it would have established him as the foremost theologian of the Reformation. But the work did not arise for merely academic reasons. We will see in Chapter Three that it arose in tribute and defense of Protestant martyrs in France.[52]

But it was this same cruelty from which he could not disentangle himself. Michael Servetus was a Spaniard, a medical doctor, a lawyer and a theologian. His doctrine of the Trinity was unorthodox—so much so that it shocked both Catholic and Protestant in his day. In 1553 he published his views and was arrested by the Catholics in France. But, alas, he escaped to Geneva. He was arrested there, and Calvin argued the case against him. He was sentenced to death. Calvin called for a swift execution, instead of burning, but he was burned at the stake on October 27, 1553.[53]

This has tarnished Calvin's name so severely that many cannot give his teaching a hearing. But it is not clear that most of us, given that milieu, would not have acted similarly under the circumstances.[54] Melanchthon was the gentle, soft-spoken associate of Martin Luther whom Calvin had met and loved. He wrote to Calvin on the Servetus affair, "I am wholly of your opinion and declare also that your magistrates acted quite justly in condemning the blasphemer to death."[55] Calvin never held civil office in Geneva[56] but exerted all his influence as a pastor. Yet, in this execution, his hands were as stained with Servetus' blood as David's were with Uriah's.

---

[52] Ibid., p. 27.
[53] Parker, *Portrait of Calvin*, p. 102.
[54] T. H. L. Parker describes some of those circumstances in ibid.
[55] Henderson, *Calvin in His Letters*, p. 196.
[56] Warfield, *Calvin and Augustine*, p. 16.

This makes the confessions of Calvin near the end of his life all the more important. On April 25, 1564, a month before his death, he called the magistrates of the city to his room and spoke these words:

> With my whole soul I embrace the mercy which [God] has exercised towards me through Jesus Christ, atoning for my sins with the merits of his death and passion, that in this way he might satisfy for *all my crimes and faults*, and blot them from his remembrance. . . . I confess I have failed innumerable times to execute my office properly, and had not He, of His boundless goodness, assisted me, all that zeal had been fleeting and vain. . . . For all these reasons, I testify and declare that I trust to no other security for my salvation than this, and this only, viz., that as God is the Father of mercy, he will show himself such a Father to me, who acknowledge myself to be *a miserable sinner*.[57]

T. H. L. Parker said, "He should never have fought the battle of faith with the world's weapons."[58] Most of us today would agree. Whether Calvin came to that conclusion before he died, we don't know. But what we know is that Calvin knew himself a "miserable sinner" whose only hope in view of "all [his] crimes" was the mercy of God and the blood of Jesus.

Why We Need the Flawed Fathers

So the times were harsh, immoral, and barbarous and had a contaminating effect on everyone, just as we are all contaminated by the evils of our own time. Their blind spots and evils may be dif-

---

[57] Dillenberger, *John Calvin, Selections from His Writings*, p. 35 (emphasis added).
[58] Parker, *Portrait of Calvin*, p. 103.

ferent from ours. And it may be that the very things they saw
clearly are the things we are blind to. It would be naive to say
that we never would have done what they did under their circumstances, and thus draw the conclusion that they have nothing to teach us. In fact, we are, no doubt, blind to many of our
evils, just as they were blind to many of theirs. The virtues they
manifested in those times are probably the very ones that we
need in ours. There was in the life and ministry of John Calvin a
grand God-centeredness, Bible-allegiance, and iron constancy.
Under the banner of God's mercy to miserable sinners, we would
do well to listen and learn. And that goes for Martin Luther and
St. Augustine as well.

The conviction behind this book is that the glory of God, however dimly, is mirrored in the flawed lives of his faithful servants.
God means for us to consider their lives and peer through the
imperfections of their faith and behold the beauty of their God.
This is what I hope will happen through the reading of this book.
There are life-giving lessons written by the hand of Divine
Providence on every page of history. The great German and the
great Frenchman drank from the great African, and God gave
the life of the Reformation.

But let us be admonished, finally, from the mouth of Luther
that the only original, true, and life-giving spring is the Word of
God. Beware of replacing the pure mountain spring of Scripture
with the sullied streams of great saints. They are precious, but they
are not pure. So we say with Luther,

> The writings of all the holy fathers should be read only
> for a time, in order that through them we may be led to the

Holy Scriptures. As it is, however, we read them only to be absorbed in them and never come to the Scriptures. We are like men who study the sign-posts and never travel the road. The dear fathers wished by their writing, to lead us to the Scriptures, but we so use them as to be led away from the Scriptures, though the Scriptures alone are our vineyard in which we ought all to work and toil.[59]

I hope it will be plain, by the focus and development of the following three chapters, that this is the design of the book: From the "Sovereign Joy" of grace discovered by Augustine to the "Sacred Study" of Scripture in the life of Luther to the "Divine Majesty of the Word" in the life and preaching of Calvin, the aim is that the glorious Gospel of God's all-satisfying, omnipotent grace will be savored, studied, and spread for the joy of all peoples—in a never-ending legacy of Soverign Joy. And so may the Lord come quickly.

---

[59] Hugh T. Kerr, *A Compend of Luther's Theology* (Philadelphia: The Westminster Press, 1943), p. 13.

How sweet all at once it was for me

to be rid of those fruitless joys

which I had once feared to lose. . . .

You drove them from me,

you who are the true, the sovereign joy.

You drove them from me and took their place,

you who are sweeter than all pleasure,

though not to flesh and blood,

you who outshine all light,

yet are hidden deeper than any secret in our hearts,

you who surpass all honor,

though not in the eyes of men who see

all honor in themselves. . . .

O Lord my God, my Light, my Wealth, and my Salvation.

St. Augustine
Confessions, IX, 1

1

SOVEREIGN JOY

The Liberating Power of Holy Pleasure in the Life and Thought of St. Augustine

The End of an Empire

On August 26, 410, the unthinkable happened. After 900 years of impenetrable security, Rome was sacked by the Gothic army led by Alaric. St. Jerome, the translator of the Latin Vulgate, was in Palestine at the time and wrote, "If Rome can perish, what can be safe?"[1] Rome did not perish immediately. It would be another sixty-six years before the Germans deposed the last Emperor. But the shock waves of the invasion reached the city of Hippo, about 450 miles southwest of Rome on the coast of North Africa, where Augustine was the bishop. He was fifty-five years old and in the prime of his ministry. He would live another twenty years and die on August 28, 430, just as 80,000 invading Vandals were about to storm the city. In other words, Augustine lived in one of those tumultuous times between the shifting of whole civilizations.

He had heard of two other Catholic bishops tortured to death in the Vandal invasion, but when his friends quoted to him the words of Jesus, "Flee to another city," he said, "Let no one dream of holding our ship so cheaply, that the sailors, let alone the Captain, should desert her in time of peril."[2] He had been the

---

[1] Peter Brown, *Augustine of Hippo* (Berkeley, CA: University of California Press, 1969), p. 289.
[2] Ibid., p. 425.

bishop of Hippo since 396 and, before that, had been a preaching elder for five years. So he had served the church for almost forty years, and was known throughout the Christian world as a God-besotted, biblical, articulate, persuasive shepherd of his flock and a defender of the faith against the great doctrinal threats of his day, mainly Manichaeism,[3] Donatism,[4] and Pelagianism.[5]

---

[3] From age nineteen to twenty-eight, Augustine was enamored with Manichaeism, but then became disillusioned with it and a great opponent in philosophical debate (Aurelius Augustine, *Confessions*, trans. R. S. Pine-Coffin [New York: Penguin Books, 1961], p. 71 [IV, 1]). Manichaeism was a heretical sect of Christianity founded by Mani, who claimed to have received an inspired message in Mesopotamia, and had been executed, in 276 A.D. by the Persian government. The "new" Christianity he founded had sloughed off the Old Testament as unspiritual and disgusting. In Mani's Christianity, "Christ did not need the witness of the Hebrew prophets: He spoke for Himself, directly to the soul, by His elevated message, by His Wisdom and His miracles. God needed no other altar than the mind" (Brown, *Augustine of Hippo*, pp. 43-44). The problem of evil was at the heart of Augustine's involvement with the Manichees. "They were dualists: so convinced were they that evil could not come from a good God, that they believed that it came from an invasion of the good—the 'Kingdom of Light'— by a hostile force of evil, equal in power, eternal, totally separate—the 'Kingdom of Darkness'" (Brown, *Augustine of Hippo*, p. 47). "The need to save an untarnished oasis of perfection within himself formed, perhaps, the deepest strain of [Augustine's] adherence to the Manichees. . . . 'For I still held the view that it was not I who was sinning, but some other nature within me'" ([*Confessions*, V, x, 18] Brown, *Augustine of Hippo*, p. 51). Augustine gives his own explanation of why he was taken by the heresy of Manichaeism: "I thought that you, Lord God who are the Truth, were a bright, unbounded body and I a small piece broken from it" (*Confessions*, p. 89 [V, 16]). "I thought that whatever had no dimension in space must be absolutely nothing at all. . . . I did not realize that the power of thought, by which I formed these images, was itself something quite different from them. And yet it could not form them unless it were itself something, and something great enough to do so" (*Confessions*, p. 134 [VII, 1]). "Because such little piety as I had compelled me to believe that God, who is good, could not have created an evil nature, I imagined that there were two antagonistic masses, both of which were infinite, yet the evil in a lesser and the good in a greater degree" (*Confessions*, p. 104 [V, 10]. From this entanglement Augustine went on to be a great apologist for the true biblical vision of one transcendent, sovereign God.

[4] Donatism "was a Christian movement of the 4th and 5th centuries, which claimed that the validity of the sacraments depends on the moral character of the minister. It arose as a result of the consecration of a bishop of Carthage in AD 311. One of the three consecrating bishops was believed to be a *traditor,* that is, one of the ecclesiastics who had been guilty of handing over their copies of the Bible to the oppressive forces of the Roman emperor Diocletian. An opposition group of 70 bishops, led by the primate of Numidia, formed itself into a synod at Carthage and declared the consecration of the bishop invalid. They held that the church must exclude from its membership persons guilty of serious sin, and that therefore no sacrament could rightly be performed by a *traditor.* The synod excommunicated the Carthaginian bishop when he refused to appear before it. Four years later, upon the death of the new bishop, the theologian Donatus the Great became bishop of Carthage; the movement later took its name from him" ("Donatism," *Microsoft® Encarta® Encyclopedia 99,* © 1993-1998 Microsoft Corporation. All rights reserved). In this controversy we see Augustine's allegiance to the sacramental character of the Catholic Church that we raised questions about in the Introduction. See pp. 26-27.

[5] The teachings of Pelagius will be explained later in this chapter.

Unparalleled and Paradoxical Influence

From this platform in North Africa, and through his remarkable faithfulness in formulating and defending the Christian faith for his generation, Augustine shaped the history of the Christian church. His influence in the Western world is simply staggering. Adolf Harnack said that he was the greatest man the church has possessed between Paul the Apostle and Luther the Reformer.[6] Benjamin Warfield argued that through his writings Augustine "entered both the Church and the world as a revolutionary force, and not merely created an epoch in the history of the Church, but . . . determined the course of its history in the West up to the present day."[7] He had "a literary talent . . . second to none in the annals of the Church."[8] "The whole development of Western life, in all its phases, was powerfully affected by his teaching."[9] The publishers of *Christian History* magazine simply say, "After Jesus and Paul, Augustine of Hippo is the most influential figure in the history of Christianity."[10]

The most remarkable thing about Augustine's influence is the fact that it flows into radically opposing religious movements. He is cherished as one of the greatest fathers of the Roman Catholic Church,[11] and yet it was Augustine who "gave us the Reformation"—not only because "Luther was an Augustinian

---

[6] Quoted from "Monasticism and the Confessions of St. Augustine," in Benjamin B. Warfield, *Calvin and Augustine* (Philadelphia: The Presbyterian and Reformed Publishing Co., 1956), p. 306.

[7] Ibid.

[8] Ibid., p. 312.

[9] Ibid., p. 310.

[10] *Christian History*, Vol. VI, No. 3, p. 2.

[11] "The Council of Orange adopted his teaching on grace, the Council of Trent his teaching on original sin and justification, and Vatican I his teaching on the relations between reason and faith. In our own day, Vatican II has made its own his teaching on the mystery of the Church and the mystery of the human person . . ." (Agostino Trapè, *Saint Augustine: Man, Pastor, Mystic* [New York: Catholic Book Publishing, 1986], p. 333).

monk, or that Calvin quoted Augustine more than any other theologian . . . [but because] the Reformation witnessed the ultimate triumph of Augustine's doctrine of grace over the legacy of
the Pelagian view of man."[12] "Both sides in the controversy
[between the Reformers and the (Catholic) counter-reformation]
appealed on a huge scale to texts of Augustine."[13]

Henry Chadwick tries to get at the scope of Augustine's influence by pointing out that "Anselm, Aquinas, Petrarch (never without a pocket copy of the *Confessions*), Luther, Bellarmine, Pascal,
and Kierkegaard all stand in the shade of his broad oak. His writings were among the favourite books of Wittgenstein. He was
the *bête noire* ["object of aversion"] of Nietzsche. His psychological analysis anticipated parts of Freud: he first discovered the
existence of the 'sub-conscious.'"[14]

There are reasons for this extraordinary influence. Agostino
Trapè gives an excellent summary of Augustine's powers that
make him incomparable in the history of the church:

> Augustine was . . . a philosopher, theologian, mystic, and
> poet in one. . . . His lofty powers complemented each other
> and made the man fascinating in a way difficult to resist.
> He is a philosopher, but not a cold thinker; he is a theolo-
> gian, but also a master of the spiritual life; he is a mystic,
> but also a pastor; he is a poet, but also a controversialist.
> Every reader thus finds something attractive and even over-
> whelming: depth of metaphysical intuition, rich abun-
> dance of theological proofs, synthetic power and energy,

[12] R. C. Sproul, "Augustine and Pelagius," in *Tabletalk*, June 1996, p. 11. "Pelagian view of man" means the view that man has the final and ultimate self-determining ability to overcome his own slavery to sin. See below in this chapter on the views of Pelagius.
[13] Henry Chadwick, *Augustine* (Oxford: Oxford University Press, 1986), p. 2.
[14] Ibid., p. 3.

psychological depth shown in spiritual ascents, and a wealth of imagination, sensibility, and mystical fervor.[15]

Visiting the Alps Without Seeing Them All

Virtually everyone who speaks or writes on Augustine has to disclaim thoroughness. Benedict Groeschel, who has written a recent introduction to Augustine, visited the Augustinian Heritage Institute adjacent to Villanova University where the books on Augustine comprise a library of their own. Then he was introduced to Augustine's five million words on computer. He speaks for many of us when he says,

> I felt like a man beginning to write a guidebook of the Swiss Alps. . . . After forty years I can still meditate on one book of the *Confessions* . . . during a week-long retreat and come back feeling frustrated that there is still so much more gold to mine in those few pages. I, for one, know that I shall never in this life escape from the Augustinian Alps.[16]

But the fact that no one can exhaust the Alps doesn't keep people from going there, even simple people. If you wonder where to start in your own reading, almost everyone would say to start with the *Confessions*, the story of Augustine's life up through his conversion and the death of his mother. The other four "great books" are: *On Christian Doctrine*; the *Enchiridion: On Faith, Hope and Love*, which, Warfield says, is "his most serious attempt to systematize his thought";[17] *On the Trinity*, which gave the

---

[15] Trapè, *Saint Augustine: Man, Pastor, Mystic*, p. 335.
[16] Benedict J. Groeschel, *Augustine: Major Writings* (New York: The Crossroad Publishing Co., 1996), pp. 1-2.
[17] Warfield, *Calvin and Augustine*, p. 307.

Trinity its definitive formulation; and *The City of God*, which was Augustine's response to the collapsing of the Empire, and his attempt to show the meaning of history.

The brevity of the tour of these Alps is drastically out of proportion to the greatness of the subject and its importance for our day. It is relevant for our ministries—whether vocational minister or layperson—and especially for the advance of the Biblical Reformed faith in our day. The title of this chapter is "Sovereign Joy: The Liberating Power of Holy Pleasure in the Life and Thought of St. Augustine." Another subtitle might have been "The Place of Pleasure in the Exposition and Defense of Evangelicalism." Or another might have been, "The Augustinian Roots of Christian Hedonism."[18]

Augustine's Life in Overview

Augustine was born in Thagaste, near Hippo, in what is now Algeria, on November 13, 354. His father, Patricius, a middle-income farmer, was not a believer. He worked hard to get Augustine the best education in rhetoric that he could, first at Madaura, twenty miles away, from age eleven to fifteen; then, after a year at home, in Carthage from age seventeen to twenty. His father was converted in 370, the year before he died, when Augustine was sixteen. He mentions his father's death only in passing one time in all his vast writings. This is all the more striking when you consider the many pages spent on the grief of losing friends.

---

[18] Christian Hedonism is the name I give to the vision of God and Christian life and ministry unfolded especially in *Desiring God, Meditations of a Christian Hedonist* (Sisters, OR: Multnomah Press, 1996).

"As I grew to manhood," he wrote, "I was inflamed with desire for a surfeit of hell's pleasures. . . . My family made no effort to save me from my fall by marriage. Their only concern was that I should learn how to make a good speech and how to persuade others by my words."[19] In particular, he said that his father "took no trouble at all to see how I was growing in your sight [O God] or whether I was chaste or not. He cared only that I should have a fertile tongue."[20] The profound disappointment in his father's care for him silenced Augustine's tongue concerning his father for the rest of his life.

Before he left for Carthage to study for three years, his mother warned him earnestly "not to commit fornication and above all not to seduce any man's wife."[21] "I went to Carthage, where I found myself in the midst of a hissing cauldron of lust. . . . My real need was for you, my God, who are the food of the soul. I was not aware of this hunger."[22] "I was willing to steal, and steal I did, although I was not compelled by any lack."[23] "I was at the top of the school of rhetoric. I was pleased with my superior status and swollen with conceit. . . . It was my ambition to be a good speaker, for the unhallowed and inane purpose of gratifying human vanity."[24] He took a concubine in Carthage and lived with this same woman for fifteen years and had one son by her, Adeodatus.

He became a traditional schoolmaster teaching rhetoric for the next eleven years of his life—age nineteen to thirty—and then

---

[19] Augustine, *Confessions*, p. 44 (II, 2).
[20] Ibid., p. 45 (II, 3).
[21] Ibid., p. 46 (II, 3).
[22] Ibid., p. 55 (III, 1).
[23] Ibid., p. 47 (II, 4).
[24] Ibid., p. 58 (III, 3).

spent the last forty-four years of his life as an unmarried monk and a bishop. Another way to say it would be that he was profligate until he was thirty-one and celibate until he was seventy-five. But his conversion was not as sudden as is often thought.

When he was nineteen, in the "cauldron of Carthage," swollen with conceit and utterly given over to sexual pleasures, he read Cicero's *Hortensius*, which for the first time arrested him by its content and not its rhetorical form. Hortensius exalted the quest for wisdom and truth above mere physical pleasure.

> It altered my outlook on life. It changed my prayers to you, O Lord, and provided me with new hopes and aspirations. All my empty dreams suddenly lost their charm and my heart began to throb with a bewildering passion for the wisdom of eternal truth. I began to climb out of the depths to which I had sunk, in order to return to you. . . . My God, how I burned with longing to have wings to carry me back to you, away from all earthly things, although I had no idea what you would do with me! For yours is the wisdom. In Greek the word "philosophy" means "love of wisdom," and it was with this love that the *Hortensius* inflamed me.[25]

This was nine years before his conversion to Christ, but it was utterly significant in redirecting his reading and thinking more toward truth rather than style, which is not a bad move in any age.

For the next nine years he was enamored by the dualistic teaching called Manichaeism, until he became disillusioned with one of its leaders when he was twenty-eight years old.[26] In his twenty-ninth year he moved from Carthage to Rome to teach, but was so fed up with the behavior of the students that he moved

---

[25] Ibid., pp. 58-59 (III, 4).
[26] Ibid., p. 71 (IV, 1).

to a teaching post in Milan, Italy, in 384. This was providential in several ways. There he would discover the Platonists, and there he would meet the great bishop Ambrose. He was now thirty years old and still had his son and his concubine—a tragic, forgotten woman whom he never once names in all his writings.

In the early summer of 386, he discovered the writings of Plotinus, a neo-Platonist[27] who had died in 270. This was Augustine's second conversion after the reading of Cicero eleven years earlier. He absorbed the Platonic vision of reality with a thrill. This encounter, Peter Brown says, "did nothing less than shift the center of gravity of Augustine's spiritual life. He was no longer identified with his God [as in Manichaeism]: This God was utterly transcendent."[28]

But he was still in the dark. You can hear the influence of his Platonism in his assessment of those days: "I had my back to the light and my face was turned towards the things which it illumined, so that my eyes, by which I saw the things which stood in the light, were themselves in darkness."[29]

Now came the time for the final move, the move from Platonism to the apostle Paul, through the tremendous impact of Ambrose who was fourteen years older than Augustine. "In Milan I found your devoted servant the bishop Ambrose. . . . At that time his gifted tongue never tired of dispensing the richness of your corn, the joy of your oil, and the sober intoxication of your wine.

---

[27] Neo-platonism was founded by Plotinus (A.D. 205-270), whose system was based chiefly on Plato's theory of Ideas. Plotinus taught that the Absolute Being is related to matter by a series of emanations through several agencies, the first of which is *nous*, or pure intelligence. From this flows the soul of the world; from this, in turn, flow the souls of humans and animals, and finally matter. Augustine would find numerous elements in this philosophy that do not cohere with biblical Christianity—for example, its categorical opposition between the spirit and matter. There was an aversion to the world of sense, and thus the necessity of liberation from a life of sense through rigorous ascetic discipline.

[28] Brown, *Augustine of Hippo*, p. 100.

[29] Augustine, *Confessions*, p. 88 (V, 16).

Unknown to me, it was you who led me to him, so that I might knowingly be led by him to you."[30]

Augustine's Platonism was scandalized by the biblical teaching that "the Word was made flesh." But week in and week out he would listen to Ambrose preach. "I was all ears to seize upon his eloquence, I also began to sense the truth of what he said, though only gradually."[31] "I thrilled with love and dread alike. I realized that I was far away from you . . . and, far off, I heard your voice saying I am the God who IS. I heard your voice, as we hear voices that speak to our hearts, and at once I had no cause to doubt."[32]

But this experience was not true conversion. "I was astonished that although I now loved you . . . I did not persist in enjoyment of my God. Your beauty drew me to you, but soon I was dragged away from you by my own weight and in dismay I plunged again into the things of this world . . . as though I had sensed the fragrance of the fare but was not yet able to eat it."[33]

Notice here the emergence of the phrase, "enjoyment of my God." Augustine now conceived of the quest of his life as a quest for a firm and unshakable enjoyment of the true God. This would be utterly determinative in his thinking about everything, especially in his great battles with Pelagianism near the end of his life forty years from this time.

He knew that he was held back now not by anything intellectual, but by sexual lust: "I was still held firm in the bonds of woman's love."[34] Therefore the battle would be determined by

[30] Ibid., p. 107 (V, 13).
[31] Ibid., p. 108 (V, 14).
[32] Ibid., p. 146 (VII, 10).
[33] Ibid., p. 152 (VII, 17).
[34] Ibid., p. 158 (VIII, 1).

the kind of pleasure that triumphed in his life. "I began to search for a means of gaining the strength I needed to enjoy you [notice the battlefront: How shall I find strength to enjoy God more than sex?], but I could not find this means until I embraced the mediator between God and men, Jesus Christ."[35]

His mother, Monica, who had prayed for him all his life, had come to Milan in the spring of 385 and had begun to arrange a proper marriage for him with a well-to-do Christian family there. This put Augustine into a heart-wrenching crisis and set him up for even deeper sin, even as his conversion was on the horizon. He sent his concubine of fifteen years back to Africa, never to live with her again. "The woman with whom I had been living was torn from my side as an obstacle to my marriage and this was a blow which crushed my heart to bleeding, because I loved her dearly. She went back to Africa, vowing never to give herself to any other man. . . . But I was too unhappy and too weak to imitate this example set me by a woman. . . . I took another mistress, without the sanction of wedlock."[36]

The History-Making Conversion

Then came one of the most important days in church history. "O Lord, my Helper and my Redeemer, I shall now tell and confess to the glory of your name how you released me from the fetters of lust which held me so tightly shackled and from my slavery to the things of this world."[37] This is the heart of his book, the *Confessions*, and one of the great works of grace in history, and

---

[35] Ibid., p. 152 (VII, 18).
[36] Ibid., p. 131 (VI, 15).
[37] Ibid., p. 166 (VIII, 6).

what a battle it was. But listen carefully how it was won. (It's recorded more fully in Book VIII of the *Confessions*.)

Even this day was more complex than the story often goes, but to go to the heart of the battle, let's focus on the final crisis. It was late August, 386. Augustine was almost thirty-two years old. With his best friend Alypius he was talking about the remarkable sacrifice and holiness of Antony, an Egyptian monk. Augustine was stung by his own bestial bondage to lust, when others were free and holy in Christ.

> There was a small garden attached to the house where we lodged. . . . I now found myself driven by the tumult in my breast to take refuge in this garden, where no one could interrupt that fierce struggle in which I was my own contestant. . . . I was beside myself with madness that would bring me sanity. I was dying a death that would bring me life. . . . I was frantic, overcome by violent anger with myself for not accepting your will and entering into your covenant. . . . I tore my hair and hammered my forehead with my fists; I locked my fingers and hugged my knees.[38]

But he began to see more clearly that the gain was far greater than the loss, and by a miracle of grace he began to see the beauty of chastity in the presence of Christ.

> I was held back by mere trifles. . . . They plucked at my garment of flesh and whispered, "Are you going to dismiss us? From this moment we shall never be with you again, for ever and ever.". . . And while I stood trembling at the barrier, on the other side I could see the chaste beauty of Continence in all her serene, unsullied joy, as she modestly

---

[38] Ibid., pp. 170-171 (VIII, 8).

beckoned me to cross over and to hesitate no more. She stretched out loving hands to welcome and embrace me.[39]

So now the battle came down to the beauty of Continence and her tenders of love versus the trifles that plucked at his flesh.

I flung myself down beneath a fig tree and gave way to the tears which now streamed from my eyes. . . . In my misery I kept crying, "How long shall I go on saying 'tomorrow, tomorrow'? Why not now? Why not make an end of my ugly sins at this moment?" . . . All at once I heard the singsong voice of a child in a nearby house. Whether it was the voice of a boy or a girl I cannot say, but again and again it repeated the refrain "Take it and read, take it and read." At this I looked up, thinking hard whether there was any kind of game in which children used to chant words like these, but I could not remember ever hearing them before. I stemmed my flood of tears and stood up, telling myself that this could only be a divine command to open my book of Scripture and read the first passage on which my eyes should fall.[40]

So I hurried back to the place where Alypius was sitting . . . seized [the book of Paul's epistles] and opened it, and in silence I read the first passage on which my eyes fell: "Not in reveling and drunkenness, not in lust and wantonness, not in quarrels and rivalries. Rather, arm yourselves with the Lord Jesus Christ; spend no more thought on nature and nature's appetites" (Romans 13:13-14). I had no wish to read more and no need to do so. For in an instant, as I came to the end of the sentence, it was as though the light of confidence flooded into my heart and all the darkness of doubt was dispelled.[41]

---

[39] Ibid., pp. 175-176 (VIII, 11).
[40] Ibid., pp. 177-178 (VIII, 12).
[41] Ibid., pp. 178 (VIII, 12).

The Unchosen Place and the Providence of God

The experience of God's grace in his own conversion set the trajectory for his theology of grace that brought him into conflict with Pelagius and made him the source of the Reformation a thousand years later. And this theology of sovereign grace was a very self-conscious theology of the triumph of joy in God.

He was baptized the next Easter, 387, in Milan by Ambrose. That autumn his mother died, a very happy woman because the son of her tears was safe in Christ. In 388 (at almost thirty-four) he returned to Africa, with a view to establishing a kind of monastery for him and his friends, whom he called "servants of God." He had given up the plan for marriage and committed himself to celibacy and poverty—that is, to the common life with others in the community.[42] He hoped for a life of philosophical leisure in the monastic way.

But God had other plans. Augustine's son, Adeodatus, died in 389. The dreams of returning to a quiet life in his hometown of Thagaste evaporated in the light of eternity. Augustine saw that it might be more strategic to move his monastic community to the larger city of Hippo. He chose Hippo because they already had a bishop, so there was less chance of his being pressed to take on that role. But he miscalculated—like Calvin more than a thousand years later. The church came to Augustine and essentially forced him to be the priest and then the bishop of Hippo, where he stayed for the rest of his life.

In a sermon much later, Augustine said to his people, "A slave may not contradict his Lord. I came to this city to see a friend,

---

[42] Brown, *Augustine of Hippo*, p. 116.

whom I thought I might gain for God, that he might live with us in the monastery. I felt secure, for the place already had a bishop. I was grabbed. I was made a priest . . . and from there, I became your bishop."[43]

And so, like so many in the history of the church who have left an enduring mark, he was thrust (at the age of thirty-six) out of a life of contemplation into a life of action. The role of bishop included settling legal disputes of church members and handling many civil affairs. "He would visit jails to protect prisoners from ill-treatment; he would intervene . . . to save criminals from judicial torture and execution; above all, he was expected to keep peace within his 'family' by arbitrating in their lawsuits."[44]

Augustine established a monastery on the grounds of the church and for almost forty years raised up a band of biblically-saturated priests and bishops who were installed all over Africa, bringing renewal to the churches. He saw himself as part of the monastery, following the strict vegetarian diet and poverty and chastity. There was an absolute prohibition on female visitors. There was too much at stake, and he knew his weakness. He never married. When he died there was no will because all his possessions belonged to the common order. His legacy was his writings, the clergy he trained, and his monastery.

The Triumph of Grace as "Sovereign Joy"

Now, back to the triumph of grace in Augustine's life and theology. Augustine experienced this grace and developed it self-consciously as a theology of "sovereign joy." R. C. Sproul says that

---

[43] Ibid., p. 138.
[44] Ibid., p. 195.

the church today is very largely in a Pelagian captivity.[45] Perhaps the prescription for the cure is for the church, and especially the lovers of God's sovereignty, to recover a healthy dose of Augustine's doctrine of "sovereign joy." Far too much Christian thinking and preaching in our day (including Reformed thinking and preaching) has not penetrated to the root of how grace actually triumphs, namely, through joy, and therefore is only half-Augustinian and half-biblical and half-beautiful.

The life and thought of Augustine bring us back to this root of joy. Pelagius was a British monk who lived in Rome in Augustine's day and taught that "though grace may facilitate the achieving of righteousness, it is not necessary to that end."[46] He denied the doctrine of original sin and asserted that human nature at its core is good and able to do all it is commanded to do. Therefore Pelagius was shocked when he read in Augustine's *Confessions*, "Give me the grace [O Lord] to do as you command, and command me to do what you will! . . . O holy God . . . when your commands are obeyed, it is from you that we receive the power to obey them."[47] Pelagius saw this as an assault on human goodness and freedom and responsibility; if God has to give what he commands, then we are not able to do what he commands and are not responsible to do what he commands, and the moral law unravels.

Augustine had not come to his position quickly. In his book *On the Freedom of the Will*, written between 388 and 391, he defended the freedom of the will in a way that caused Pelagius to

---

[45] "What would Luther think of the modern heirs of the Reformation? My guess is that he would write on the modern church's captivity to Pelagianism," R. C. Sproul, *Willing to Believe: The Controversy Over Free Will* (Grand Rapids: Baker Books, 1997), p. 21.

[46] Sproul, "Augustine and Pelagius," p. 13.

[47] Augustine, *Confessions*, p. 236 (X, 31).

quote Augustine's own book against him in later life.[48] But by the time Augustine wrote the *Confessions* ten years later, the issue was settled. Here is what he wrote (this may be one of the most important paragraphs for understanding the heart of Augustine's thought, and the essence of Augustinianism):

> During all those years [of rebellion], where was my free will? What was the hidden, secret place from which it was summoned in a moment, so that I might bend my neck to your easy yoke? . . . How sweet all at once it was for me to be rid of *those fruitless joys* which I had once feared to lose! . . . *You drove them from me*, you who are the true, the *sovereign joy*. [There's the key phrase and the key reality for understanding the heart of Augustinianism.] You drove them from me and took their place, you who are *sweeter than all pleasure*, though not to flesh and blood, you who outshine all light, yet are hidden deeper than any secret in our hearts, you who surpass all honor, though not in the eyes of men who see all honor in themselves. . . . O Lord my God, my Light, my Wealth, and my Salvation.[49]

This is Augustine's understanding of grace. *Grace is God's giving us sovereign joy in God that triumphs over joy in sin.* In other words, God works deep in the human heart to transform the springs of joy so that we love God more than sex or anything else. Loving God, in Augustine's mind, is never reduced to deeds of obedience or acts of willpower. He never makes the mistake of quoting John 14:15 ("If you love Me, you will keep My commandments") and claiming that love *is* the same as keeping

---

[48] "So, paradoxically the great opponent of Augustine's old age had been inspired by those treatises of the young philosopher, in which Augustine had defended the freedom of the will against a Manichaean determinism" (Brown, *Augustine of Hippo*, p. 149).

[49] Augustine, *Confessions*, p. 181 (IX, 1), emphasis added.

Christ's commandments, when the text says that keeping Christ's commandments *results from* loving Christ. "*If* you love, *then* me you will obey." Nor does he make the mistake of quoting 1 John 5:3 ("For this is the love of God, that we keep His commandments; and His commandments are not burdensome") and overlook the point that loving God means keeping his commandments *in such a way* that his commandments are not burdensome. Loving God is being so satisfied in God and so delighted in all that he is for us that his commandments cease to be burdensome. Augustine saw this. And we need him badly today to help us recover the root of all Christian living in the triumphant joy in God that dethrones the sovereignty of laziness and lust and greed.

For Augustine, loving God is always a delighting in God, and in other things only for God's sake. He defines it clearly in *On Christian Doctrine* (III, x, 16). "I call 'charity' [i.e., love for God] the motion of the soul toward the enjoyment of God for His own sake, and the enjoyment of one's self and of one's neighbor for the sake of God."[50] Loving God is always conceived of essentially as delighting in God and in anything else for his sake.

Augustine analyzed his own motives down to this root. Everything springs from delight. He saw this as a universal: "Every man, whatsoever his condition, desires to be happy. There is no man who does not desire this, and each one desires it with such earnestness that he prefers it to all other things; whoever, in fact, desires other things, desires them for this end alone."[51] This

[50] St. Augustine, *On Christian Doctrine*, trans. D. W. Robertson, Jr. (Upper Saddle River, NJ: Prentice Hall, 1958), p. 88. He adds, "'Cupidity' is a motion of the soul toward the enjoyment of one's self, one's neighbor, or any corporal thing for the sake of something other than God."

[51] Thomas A. Hand, *Augustine on Prayer* (New York: Catholic Book Publishing Co., 1986), p. 13 (Sermon 306). See Augustine, *Confessions*, p. 228 (X, 21): "Without exception we all long for happiness . . . all agree that they want to be happy. . . . They may all search for it in different ways, but all try their hardest to reach the same goal, that is, joy."

is what guides and governs the will, namely, what we consider to be our delight.

But here's the catch that made Pelagius so angry. Augustine believed that it is not in our power to determine what this delight will be.

> Who has it in his power to have such a motive present to his mind that his will shall be influenced to believe? Who can welcome in his mind something which does not give him delight? But who has it in his power to ensure that something that will delight him will turn up? Or that he will take delight in what turns up? If those things delight us which serve our advancement towards God, that is due not to our own whim or industry or meritorious works, but to the inspiration of God and to the grace which he bestows.[52]

So saving grace, converting grace, in Augustine's view, is *God's giving us a sovereign joy in God* that triumphs over all other joys and therefore sways the will. The will is free to move toward whatever it delights in most fully, but it is not within the power of our will to determine what that *sovereign joy* will be. Therefore Augustine concludes,

> A man's free-will, indeed, avails for nothing except to sin, if he knows not the way of truth; and even after his duty

---

[52] T. Kermit Scott, *Augustine: His Thought in Context* (New York: Paulist Press, 1995), p. 203 (*To Simplician*, II, 21). In another place he said, "Clearly it is in vain for us to will unless God have mercy. But I don't know how it could be said that it is vain for God to have mercy unless we willingly consent. If God has mercy, we also will, for the power to will is given with the mercy itself. It is God that worketh in us both to will and to do of his good pleasure. If we ask whether a good will is a gift of God, I should be surprised if anyone would venture to deny that. But because the good will does not precede calling, but calling precedes the good will, the fact that we have a good will is rightly attributed to God who calls us, and the fact that we are called cannot be attributed to our selves" (Scott, *Augustine: His Thought in Context*, p. 201 [*To Simplician* II, 12]).

and his proper aim shall begin to become known to him,
unless he also take delight in and feel a love for it, he neither does his duty, nor sets about it, nor lives rightly. Now,
in order that such a course may engage our affections,
God's "love is shed abroad in our hearts" not through
the free-will which arises from ourselves, but "through
the Holy Ghost, which is given to us" (Romans 5:5).[53]

In 427, he looked back over a lifetime of thought on this
issue and wrote to Simplician, "In answering this question I have
tried hard to maintain the free choice of the human will, but
the grace of God prevailed."[54] Controversy was Augustine's daily
vocation. Near the end of his life, he listed over eighty heresies
that he had fought against.[55] Why this defensive labor, in view
of his deepest longing for joy in God? He gives one answer in the
Confessions: "It is indeed true that the refutation of heretics
gives greater prominence to the tenets of your Church [O Lord]
and the principles of sound doctrine. For parties there must
needs be, so that those who are true metal may be distinguished
from the rest."[56]

But there was a deeper reason for his long engagement in the
Pelagian controversy. When he was asked by his friend Paulinus
why he kept on investing so much energy in this dispute with
Pelagius, even as a man in his seventies, he answered, "First and
foremost because no subject [but grace] gives me greater pleasure. For what ought to be more attractive to us sick men, than

---

[53] Scott, *Augustine: His Thought in Context*, p. 208 (*Spirit and Letter*, V).

[54] Scott, *Augustine: His Thought in Context*, p. 211 (*To Simplician*, II, 1).

[55] Augustine wrote *On Heresies* during 428-429 and it remains unfinished because of his death. In it he lists over eighty heresies from Simon Magus to the Pelagians (Brown, *Augustine of Hippo*, pp. 35-56).

[56] Augustine, *Confessions*, pp. 153-154 (VII, 19).

grace, grace by which we are healed; for us lazy men, than grace, grace by which we are stirred up; for us men longing to act, than grace, by which we are helped?"[57] This answer has all the more power when you keep in mind that all the healing, stirring, helping, enabling grace that Augustine revels in is *the giving of a compelling, triumphant joy*. Grace governs life by giving a supreme joy in the supremacy of God.

Augustine is utterly committed to the moral accountability of the human will, even though the will is ultimately governed by the delights of the soul that are ordered finally by God. When pressed for an explanation, he is willing, in the end, to rest with Scripture in a "profound mystery." This can be seen in the following two quotes:

> Now, should any man be for constraining us to examine into this profound mystery, why this person is so persuaded as to yield, and that person is not, there are only two things occurring to me, which I should like to advance as my answer: "O the depth of the riches!" (Romans 11:33) and "Is there unrighteousness with God?" (Romans 9:14). If the man is displeased with such an answer, he must seek more learned disputants: but let him beware lest he find presumptuousness.[58]

> Let this truth, then, be fixed and unmovable in a mind soberly pious and stable in faith, that there is no unrighteousness with God. Let us also believe most firmly and tenaciously that God has mercy on whom he will and that whom he will he hardeneth, that is, he has or has not mercy on whom he will. Let us believe that this belongs

---

[57] Brown, *Augustine of Hippo*, p. 355 (Epistle 186, XII, 139).
[58] Scott, *Augustine: His Thought in Context*, pp. 209-210 (*Spirit and Letter*, LX).

to a certain hidden equity that cannot be searched out by any human standard of measurement, though its effects are to be observed in human affairs and earthly arrangements.[59]

The fact that grace governs life by giving a supreme joy in the supremacy of God explains why the concept of Christian freedom is so radically different in Augustine than in Pelagius. For Augustine freedom is to be so much in love with God and his ways that the very experience of choice is transcended. The ideal of freedom is not the autonomous will poised with sovereign equilibrium between good and evil. The ideal of freedom is to be so spiritually discerning of God's beauty, and to be so in love with God that one never stands with equilibrium between God and an alternate choice. Rather, one transcends the experience of choice and walks under the continual sway of sovereign joy in God. In Augustine's view, the self-conscious experience of having to contemplate choices was a sign not of the freedom of the will, but of the disintegration of the will. The struggle of choice is a necessary evil in this fallen world until the day comes when discernment and delight unite in a perfect apprehension of what is infinitely delightful, namely, God.

What follows from Augustine's view of grace as the giving of a sovereign joy that triumphs over "lawless pleasures"[60] is that the entire Christian life is seen as a relentless quest for the fullest joy in God. He said, "The whole life of a good Christian is a holy

---

[59] Scott, *Augustine: His Thought in Context*, p. 212 (*To Simplician*, II, 16).

[60] Augustine, *Confessions*, p. 44 (II, 2). "You were always present, angry and merciful at once, strewing the pangs of bitterness over all my lawless pleasures to lead me on to look for others unallied with pain. You meant me to find them nowhere but in yourself, O Lord, for you teach us by inflicting pain, you smite so that you may heal, and you kill us so that we may not die away from you."

desire."[61] In other words, the key to Christian living is a thirst and a hunger for God. And one of the main reasons people do not understand or experience the sovereignty of grace and the way it works through the awakening of sovereign joy is that their hunger and thirst for God is so small. The desperation to be ravished for the sake of worship and holiness is unintelligible. Here's the goal and the problem as Augustine saw it:

> The soul of men shall hope under the shadow of Thy wings; they shall be made drunk with the fullness of Thy house; and of the torrents of Thy pleasures Thou wilt give them to drink; for in Thee is the Fountain of Life, and in Thy Light shall we see the light? Give me a man in love: he knows what I mean. Give me one who yearns; give me one who is hungry; give me one far away in this desert, who is thirsty and sighs for the spring of the Eternal country. Give me that sort of man: he knows what I mean. But if I speak to a cold man, he just does not know what I am talking about. . . .[62]

These words from Augustine should make our hearts burn with renewed longing for God. And they should help us see why it is so difficult to display the glory of the Gospel to so many people. The reason is that so many do not long for anything very much. They are just coasting. They are not passionate about anything. They are "cold" not just toward the glory of Christ in the Gospel, but toward everything. Even their sins are picked at rather than swallowed with passion.

---

[61] Hand, *Augustine on Prayer*, p. 20 (*Treatise on 1 John* 4:6).
[62] Brown, *Augustine of Hippo*, pp. 374-375 (*Tractatus in Joannis evangelium*, 26, 4).

The Place of Prayer in the Pursuit of Joy

The remedy from God's side for this condition of "coldness," of course, is the gracious awakening of a sovereign joy. But on the human side, it is prayer and the display of God himself as infinitely more desirable than all creation. It is not a mere stylistic device that all 350 pages of the *Confessions* are written as a prayer. Every sentence is addressed to God. This is astonishing. It must have required enormous literary discipline not to fall into some other form. The point of this discipline is that Augustine is utterly dependent on God for the awakening of love to God. And it is no coincidence that the prayers of Augustine's mother Monica pervade the *Confessions*. She pled for him when he would not plead for himself.[63]

Augustine counsels us, "Say with the psalmist: 'One thing I ask of the Lord, this I seek: To dwell in the house of the Lord all the days of my life, that I may gaze on the loveliness of the Lord and contemplate his temple' (Psalm 27:4)." Then he says, "In order that we may attain this happy life, he who is himself the true Blessed Life has taught us to pray."[64] Augustine shows us the way he prayed for the triumph of joy in God: "O Lord, that I may love you [freely], for I can find nothing more precious. Turn not away your face from me, that I may find what I seek. Turn not aside in anger from your servant, lest in seeking you I run toward something else. . . . Be my helper. Leave me not, neither despise me, O God my Saviour."[65]

His mother's praying became the school where he learned

---

[63] See notes 67, 69, 70.
[64] Hand, *Augustine on Prayer*, p. 25 (*Letter 130*, 15).
[65] Ibid., p. 27.

deep things about Jesus' words in John 16:24, "Until now you have asked for nothing in My name; ask, and you will receive, so that your joy may be made full." Prayer is the path to fullness of sovereign joy. But, oh, what a strange and circuitous path! Monica had learned patience in the pain of long-unanswered prayers. For example, her husband, Patricius, was unfaithful to her. But Augustine recalls in the *Confessions* that "her patience was so great that his infidelity never became a cause of quarreling between them. For she looked to you to show him mercy, hoping that chastity would come with faith. . . . In the end she won her husband for you [O Lord] as a convert in the very last days of his life on earth."[66]

So it would prove to be with her son. She "shed more tears [over] my spiritual death," Augustine said, "than other mothers shed for the bodily death of a son."[67] When her son was a Manichaean heretic, Monica sought help from an old bishop. His counsel was not what she wanted to hear: He too had been a Manichee once, but had seen his folly. "Leave him alone," he said. "Just pray to God for him. From his own reading he will discover his mistakes and the depth of his profanity. . . . Leave me and go in peace. It cannot be that the son of these tears should be lost."[68]

At the age of sixteen in 371, soon after his father's death, Augustine sneaked away from his mother in Carthage and sailed to Rome. "During the night, secretly, I sailed away, leaving her alone to her tears and her prayers."[69] How were these prayers answered? Not the way Monica hoped at that time. Only later could she see

---

[66] Augustine, *Confessions*, pp. 194-195.
[67] Ibid., p. 68 (III, 11).
[68] Ibid., pp. 69-70 (III, 12).
[69] Ibid., p. 101 (V, 8).

the truth of Jesus' words worked out in her life—that praying is the path to deepest joy. "And what did she beg of you, my God, with all those tears, if not that you would prevent me from sailing? But you did not do as she asked you. Instead, in the depth of your wisdom, you granted the wish that was closest to her heart. You did with me what she had always asked you to do."[70]

Later, just after his conversion, he went to tell his mother what God had done in answer to her prayers:

> Then we went and told my mother [of my conversion], who was overjoyed. And when we went on to describe how it had all happened, she was jubilant with triumph and glorified you, who are powerful enough, and more than powerful enough, to carry out your purpose beyond all our hopes and dreams. For she saw that you had granted her far more than she used to ask in her tearful prayers and plaintive lamentations. You converted me to yourself, so that I no longer desired a wife or placed any hope in this world but stood firmly upon the rule of faith, where you had shown me to her in a dream years before. And you turned her sadness into rejoicing, into joy far fuller than her dearest wish, far sweeter and more chaste than any she had hoped to find in children begotten of my flesh.[71]

Such was the lesson Augustine learned from the unremitting travail of his mother's prayers. Not what she thought she wanted in the short run, but what she most deeply wanted in the long run—God gave her "joy far fuller than her dearest wish." "Ask, and you will receive, so that your joy may be made full" (John 16:24).

---

[70] Ibid.
[71] Ibid., pp. 178-179 (VIII, 12).

Displaying the Superior Delight of Knowing God

But alongside prayer, the remedy for people without passion and without hunger and thirst for God is to display God himself as infinitely more desirable—more satisfying— than all creation. Augustine's zeal for the souls of men and women was that they might come to see the beauty of God and love him. "If your delight is in souls, love them in God . . . and draw as many with you to him as you can."[72] "You yourself [O God] are their joy. Happiness is to rejoice in you and for you and because of you. This is true happiness and there is no other."[73]

So Augustine labored with all his spiritual and poetic and intellectual might to help people see and feel the all-satisfying supremacy of God over all things.

> But what do I love when I love my God? . . . Not the sweet melody of harmony and song; not the fragrance of flowers, perfumes, and spices; not manna or honey; not limbs such as the body delights to embrace. It is not these that I love when I love my God. And yet, when I love him, it is true that I love a light of a certain kind, a voice, a perfume, a food, an embrace; but they are of the kind that I love in my inner self, when my soul is bathed in light that is not bound by space; when it listens to sound that never dies away; when it breathes fragrance that is not borne away on the wind; when it tastes food that is never consumed by the eating; when it clings to an embrace from which it is not severed by fulfillment of desire. This is what I love when I love my God.[74]

---

[72] Ibid., p. 82 (IV, 12).
[73] Ibid., p. 228 (X, 22).
[74] Ibid., pp. 211-212 (X, 6).

Few people in the history of the church have surpassed Augustine in portraying the greatness and beauty and desirability of God. He is utterly persuaded by Scripture and experience "that he is happy who possesses God."[75] "You made us for yourself, and our hearts find no peace till they rest in you."[76] He will labor with all his might to make this God of sovereign grace and sovereign joy known and loved in the world.

> You are ever active, yet always at rest. You gather all things to yourself, though you suffer no need. . . . You grieve for wrong, but suffer no pain. You can be angry and yet serene. Your works are varied, but your purpose is one and the same. . . . You welcome those who come to you, though you never lost them. You are never in need yet are glad to gain, never covetous yet you exact a return for your gifts. . . . You release us from our debts, but you lose nothing thereby. You are my God, my Life, my holy Delight, but is this enough to say of you? Can any man say enough when he speaks of you? Yet woe betide those who are silent about you![77]

What a preacher Augustine became in his passion not to be "silent" about the all-satisfying pleasures at God's right hand! "Can any man say enough when he speaks of you?" He explained to his own congregation how his preaching came to be: "I go to feed [myself] so that I can give you to eat. I am the servant, the bringer of food, not the master of the house. I lay out before you that from which I also draw my life."[78] This was his way of study: he sought for soul-food that he might feed himself on God's "holy Delight" and then feed his people.

[75] Hand, *Augustine on Prayer*, p. 17 (*On the Happy Life*, 11).
[76] Augustine, *Confessions*, p. 21 (I, 1).
[77] Ibid., p. 23 (I, 4).
[78] Brown, *Augustine of Hippo*, p. 252 (Epistle 73, II, 5).

Even his ability—and his hearers' ability—to see the truth of Scripture was governed partially by the delight he took in what he found there. He would always tell his readers that they must "look into the Scriptures [with] the eyes of their heart on its heart." This means that one must look with love on what one only partially sees: "It is impossible to love what is entirely unknown, but when what is known, if even so little, is loved, this very capacity for love makes it better and more fully known."[79] In other words, loving, or delighting in, what we know of God in Scripture will be the key that opens Scripture further. So study and preaching were, for Augustine, anything but detached and impartial, as scholarship is so often conceived today.

He explained to the great Bible scholar Jerome that he could therefore never be a "disinterested" scholar, because "If I do gain any stock of knowledge [in the Scriptures], I pay it out immediately to the people of God."[80] And what was it that he showed them and fed them? It was the very joy that he himself found in God: "The thread of our speech comes alive through the very joy we take in what we are speaking about."[81] That was the key to his preaching, and the key to his life—he could not cease seeking and speaking about the sovereign joy in God that had set him free by the power of a superior satisfaction.

The Unchanged Relevance of Grace As "Sovereign Joy"

The implications of Augustine's experience and his theology of sovereign joy are tremendously relevant not only for preaching

---

[79] Ibid., p. 279 (*Tractatus in Joannis evangelium*, 96, 4).
[80] Ibid., p. 252 (Epistle 73, II, 5).
[81] Ibid., p. 256.

but also for evangelism. What had happened to him can happen to others because every human heart is the same in this way. "I am not alone in this desire [for the blessed state of happiness], nor are there only a few who share it with me: without exception we all long for happiness. . . . All agree that they want to be happy. . . . They may all search for it in different ways, but all try their hardest to reach the same goal, that is, joy."[82] This is a great common ground for doing evangelism in every age. Deeper than all "felt needs" is the real need: God. Not just God experienced without emotional impact, but rather God experienced as "holy Delight." "You made us for yourself, and our hearts find no peace till they rest in you."[83] This peace is the presence of a profound happiness. "He is happy who possesses God."[84] Not because God gives health, wealth, and prosperity, but because God *is* our soul's joyful resting place. To make this known and experienced through Jesus Christ is the goal of evangelism and world missions.

Augustine's doctrine of delight in God is the root of all Christian living. He brings it to bear on the most practical affairs of life and shows that every moment in every circumstance we stand on the brink between the lure of idolatry and the delight of seeing and knowing God. Perhaps he erred on the side of asceticism at times in an overreaction to the lust of his youth. But in principle he seemed to get it right. For example, his chief rule on using the things of the world so that they are gratefully received as God's gifts but do not become idols is expressed in this prayer:

[82] Augustine, *Confessions*, p. 228 (X, 21).
[83] Ibid., p. 21 (I, 1).
[84] Hand, *Augustine on Prayer*, p. 17 (*On the Happy Life*, 11).

"He loves thee too little who loves anything together with thee, which he loves not for thy sake."[85] He illustrates:

> Suppose, brethren, a man should make a ring for his betrothed, and she should love the ring more wholeheartedly than the betrothed who made it for her. . . . Certainly, let her love his gift: but, if she should say, "The ring is enough. I do not want to see his face again" what would we say of her? . . . The pledge is given her by the betrothed just that, in his pledge, he himself may be loved. God, then, has given you all these things. Love Him who made them.[86]

Instead of minimizing the greatness and the beauty of this world, Augustine admired it and made it a means of longing for the City of which this is all a shadow. "From His gifts, which are scattered to good and bad alike in this, our most grim life, let us, with His help, try to express sufficiently what we have yet to experience."[87] He ponders the wonders of the human body and the "gratuitous ornament of a male beard," and even turns admiringly to pagan scholarship: "Who can possibly do full justice to the intellectual brilliance displayed by philosophers and heretics in defending their errors and incorrect opinions?"[88]

His delight in nature comes out in this regard as he, perhaps, looks out over the Bay of Hippo: "There is the grandeur of the spectacle of the sea itself, as it slips on and off its many colors like robes, and now is all shades of green, now purple, now sky-blue. . . . And all these are mere consolations for us, for us

---

[85] Quoted in *Documents of the Christian Church*, Henry Bettenson, ed. (London: Oxford University Press, 1967), p. 54.

[86] Brown, *Augustine of Hippo*, p. 326 (*Tractate on the Epistle of John*, 2:11).

[87] Ibid., p. 328 (*City of God*, XXII, 21, 26).

[88] Ibid., p. 329 (*City of God*, XXII, 24 160).

unhappy, punished men: they are not the rewards of the blessed. What can these be like then, if such things here are so many, so great, and of such a quality?"[89] Augustine's relentless focus on the City of God did not prevent him from seeing the beauties of this world and enjoying them for what they are—good gifts of God pointing us ever to the Giver and the superior joys of his presence. We need to heed the unremitting call of Augustine to be free from the ensnaring delights of this world, not because they are evil in themselves, but because so few of us use them as we ought: "If the things of this world delight you, praise God for them but turn your love away from them and give it to their Maker, so that in the things that please you may not displease him."[90]

Augustine's vision of salvation through Jesus Christ and of living the Christian life is rooted in his understanding and experience of grace—the divine gift of triumphant joy in God. The power that saves and sanctifies is the work of God deep beneath the human will to transform the springs of joy so that we love God more than sex or seas or scholarship or food or friends or fame or family or money. Grace is the key because it is free and creates a new heart with new delights that govern the will and the work of our lives. "It does not depend on the man who wills or the man who runs, but on God who has mercy" (Romans 9:16).

If it is true, as R. C. Sproul says, that today "we have not broken free from the Pelagian captivity of the church"[91]—a captivity that Augustine warred against for so many years for the sake of sovereign joy—then we should pray and preach and write and teach and labor with all our might to break the chain

---

[89] Ibid., p. 329 (*City of God*, XXII 24, 175).
[90] Augustine, *Confessions*, p. 82 (IV, 12).
[91] R. C. Sproul, "Augustine and Pelagius," p. 52.

that holds us captive. Sproul says, "We need an Augustine or a Luther to speak to us anew lest the light of God's grace be not only overshadowed but be obliterated in our time."[92] Yes, we do. But we also need tens of thousands of ordinary pastors and laypeople who are ravished with the extraordinary power of joy in God.

And we need to rediscover Augustine's peculiar slant—a very biblical slant—on grace as the free gift of sovereign joy in God that frees us from the bondage of sin. We need to rethink our Reformed doctrine of salvation so that every limb and every branch in the tree is coursing with the sap of Augustinian delight. We need to make plain that *total depravity* is not just badness, but blindness to beauty and deadness to joy; and *unconditional election* means that the completeness of our joy in Jesus was planned for us before we ever existed; and that *limited atonement* is the assurance that indestructible joy in God is infallibly secured for us by the blood of the covenant; and *irresistible grace* is the commitment and power of God's love to make sure we don't hold on to suicidal pleasures, and to set us free by the sovereign power of superior delights; and that the *perseverance of the saints* is the almighty work of God to keep us, through all affliction and suffering, for an inheritance of pleasures at God's right hand forever.

This note of sovereign, triumphant joy is a missing element in too much Christian (especially Reformed) theology and worship. Maybe the question we should pose ourselves is whether this is so because we have not experienced the triumph of sovereign joy in our own lives. Can we say the following with Augustine?

---

[92] Ibid.

How sweet all at once it was for me to be rid of *those fruitless joys* which I had once feared to lose! . . . *You drove them from me*, you who are the true, the *sovereign joy*. You drove them from me and took their place. . . . O Lord my God, my Light, my Wealth, and my Salvation.[93]

Or are we in bondage to the pleasures of this world so that, for all our talk about the glory of God, we love television and food and sleep and sex and money and human praise just like everybody else? If so, let us repent and fix our faces like flint toward the Word of God. And let us pray: O Lord, open my eyes to see the sovereign sight that in your presence is fullness of joy and at your right hand are pleasures forevermore (Psalm 16:11). Grant, O God, that we would live the legacy of Sovereign Joy.

---

[93] Augustine, *Confessions*, p. 181 (IX, 1), emphasis added.

In this psalm [119] David always says that he will speak, think,

talk, hear, read, day and night and constantly—but about nothing

else than God's Word and Commandments. For God wants to give

you His Spirit only through the external Word.

MARTIN LUTHER
PREFACE TO HIS *1539* WORKS

It is a sin and shame not to know our own book or to understand

the speech and words of our God; it is a still greater sin and loss

that we do not study languages, especially in these days when God

is offering and giving us men and books and every facility and

inducement to this study, and desires his Bible to be an open book.

O how happy the dear fathers would have been if they had our

opportunity to study the languages and come thus prepared to the

Holy Scriptures! What great toil and effort it cost them to gather

up a few crumbs, while we with half the labor—yes, almost

without any labor at all—can acquire the whole loaf! O how their

effort puts our indolence to shame!

MARTIN LUTHER
"TO THE COUNCILMEN OF ALL CITIES IN GERMANY THAT
THEY ESTABLISH AND MAINTAIN CHRISTIAN SCHOOLS"

2

SACRED STUDY

Martin Luther and the External Word

The Word of God Is a Book

One of the great rediscoveries of the Reformation—especially of Martin Luther—was that the Word of God comes to us in the form of a book. In other words, Luther grasped this powerful fact: God preserves the experience of salvation and holiness from generation to generation by means of a book of revelation, not a bishop in Rome, and not the ecstasies of Thomas Muenzer and the Zwickau prophets.[1] The Word of God comes to us in a book. This rediscovery shaped Luther and the Reformation.

One of Luther's arch-opponents in the Roman Church, Sylvester Prierias, wrote in response to Luther's 95 theses (posted in 1517): "He who does not accept the doctrine of the Church of Rome and pontiff of Rome as an infallible rule of faith, from which the Holy Scriptures, too, draw their strength and authority, is a heretic."[2] In other words, the Church and the pope are

---

[1] Thomas Muenzer, seven years Luther's junior, became the preacher at the Church of St. Mary in Zwickau. "He . . . joined a union of fanatics, mostly weavers, who, with Nikolaus Storch at their head, had organized themselves under the leadership of twelve apostles and seventy-two disciples, and held secret conventicles, in which they pretended to receive divine revelations" (Philip Schaff, ed., *Religious Encyclopedia*, vol. 2 [New York: The Christian Literature Co., 1888], p. 1596). For Luther's response, see A. G. Dickens and Alun Davies, eds., *Documents of Modern History: Martin Luther* (New York: St. Martin's Press, 1970), pp. 75-79.

[2] Heiko A. Oberman, *Luther: Man Between God and the Devil*, trans. Eileen Walliser-Schwarzbart (New York: Doubleday, 1992, orig. 1982), p. 193. Professor Steven Ozment of Harvard calls Heiko Oberman "the world's foremost authority on Luther."

the authoritative deposit of salvation and the Word of God; and the book—the Bible—is derivative and secondary. "What is new in Luther," Heiko Oberman says, "is the notion of absolute obedience to the Scriptures against any authorities; be they popes or councils."[3] In other words, the saving, sanctifying, authoritative Word of God comes to us in a book. The implications of this simple observation are tremendous.

In 1539, commenting on Psalm 119, Luther wrote, "In this psalm David always says that he will speak, think, talk, hear, read, day and night and constantly—but about nothing else than God's Word and Commandments. *For God wants to give you His Spirit only through the external Word.*"[4] This phrase is extremely important. The "external Word" is the book. And the saving, sanctifying, illuminating Spirit of God, he says, comes to us *through* this "external Word." Luther calls it the "external Word" to emphasize that it is objective, fixed, outside ourselves, and therefore unchanging. It is a book. Neither ecclesiastical hierarchy nor fanatical ecstasy can replace it or shape it. It is "external," like God. You can take or leave it. But you can't make it other than what it is. It is a book with fixed letters and words and sentences.

Luther said with resounding forcefulness in 1545, the year before he died, "Let the man who would hear God speak, read Holy Scripture."[5] Earlier he had said in his lectures on Genesis, "The Holy Spirit himself and God, the Creator of all things, is the Author of this book."[6] One of the implications of the fact that the Word of God comes to us in a book is that the theme of

---

[3] Ibid., p. 204.
[4] Ewald M. Plass, compiler, *What Luther Says: An Anthology*, vol. 3 (St. Louis: Concordia Publishing House, 1959), p. 1359 (emphasis added).
[5] Plass, *What Luther Says*, vol. 2, p. 62.
[6] Ibid.

this chapter is "The Pastor and His Study," not "The Pastor and His Seance" or "The Pastor and His Intuition" or "The Pastor and His Religious Multi-perspectivalism." The Word of God that saves and sanctifies, from generation to generation, is preserved in a book. And therefore at the heart of every pastor's work is book-work. Call it reading, meditation, reflection, cogitation, study, exegesis, or whatever you will—a large and central part of our work is to wrestle God's meaning from a book, and then to proclaim it in the power of the Holy Spirit.

Luther knew that some would stumble over the sheer conservatism of this simple, unchangeable fact: God's Word is fixed in a book. He knew then, as we know today, that many say this assertion nullifies or minimizes the crucial role of the Holy Spirit in giving life and light. Luther would probably say, "Yes, that might happen. One might argue that emphasizing the brightness of the sun nullifies the surgeon who takes away blindness." But most people would not agree with that. Certainly not Luther.

He said in 1520, "Be assured that no one will make a doctor of the Holy Scripture save only the Holy Ghost from heaven."[7] Luther was a great lover of the Holy Spirit. And his exaltation of the book as the "external Word" did not belittle the Spirit. On the contrary, it elevated the Spirit's great gift to Christendom. In 1533 Luther said, "The Word of God is the greatest, most necessary, and most important thing in Christendom."[8] Without the "external Word" we would not know one spirit from the other, and the objective personality of the Holy Spirit himself would be lost in a blur of subjective expressions. Cherishing the book

[7] Plass, *What Luther Says,* vol. 3, p. 1355.
[8] Plass, *What Luther Says,* vol. 2, p. 913.

implied to Luther that the Holy Spirit is a beautiful person to be known and loved, not a buzz to be felt.

Another objection to Luther's emphasis on the book is that it minimizes the incarnate Word, Jesus Christ himself. Luther says the opposite is true. To the degree that the Word of God is disconnected from the objective, "external Word," to that degree the incarnate Word, the historical Jesus, becomes a wax nose shaped by the preferences of every generation. Luther had one weapon with which to rescue the incarnate Word from being sold in the markets of Wittenberg. He drove out the money changers—the indulgence sellers—with the whip of the "external Word," the book.

When he posted the 95 theses on October 31, 1517, thesis 45 read, "Christians should be taught that he who sees someone needy but looks past him, and buys an indulgence instead, receives not the pope's remission but God's wrath."[9] That blow fell from the book—from the story of the Good Samaritan and from the second great commandment in the book, the "external Word." Without the book there would have been no blow, and the incarnate Word would be everybody's clay toy. So precisely for the sake of the incarnate Word Luther exalts the written Word, the "external Word."

It is true that the church needs to *see* the Lord in his earthly talking and walking on the earth. Our faith is rooted in that decisive revelation in history. But Luther reasserted that this *seeing* happens through a written record. The incarnate Word is revealed to us in a book.[10] Is it not remarkable that the Spirit in Luther's

---

[9] Oberman, *Luther: Man Between God and the Devil*, p. 77.

[10] It is true that "flesh and blood" cannot see the glory of the Lord (Matthew 16:17). Only the Spirit of God can open the eyes of the heart to see the glory of God in the face of Christ (2 Corinthians 4:6). I am not denying that. I only mean, with Luther, that the Spirit does not reveal the Son apart from the "external Word."

day, and in our day, was and is virtually silent about the history of the incarnate Lord on the earth—except in amplifying the glory of the Lord through the written record of the incarnate Word?

That is, neither the Roman Catholic Church nor charismatic prophets claimed that the Spirit of the Lord narrated to them untold events of the historical Jesus. This is astonishing. Of all the claims to authority *over* the "external Word" (by the pope) and *alongside* the "external Word" (by contemporary prophets), none of them brings forth new information about the incarnate life and ministry of Jesus. Rome will dare to add facts to the life of Mary (for example, the immaculate conception[11]), but not to the life of Jesus. Charismatic prophets will announce new movements of the Lord in the sixteenth century, and in our day, but none seems to report a new parable or a new miracle of the incarnate Word omitted from the Gospels—in spite of the fact that the apostle John wrote, "There are also many other things which Jesus did, which if they were written in detail, I suppose that even the world itself would not contain the books which were written" (John 21:25). Neither Roman authority nor prophetic ecstasy adds to or deletes from the external record of the incarnate Word.[12]

Why is the Spirit so silent about the incarnate Word after the age of the New Testament—even among those who encroach on the authority of the book? The answer seems to be that it pleased God

---

[11] Pope Pius IX announced the doctrine on December 8, 1854, with these words: "That the most blessed Virgin Mary, in the first moment of her conception, by a special grace and privilege of Almighty God, in virtue of the merits of Christ, was preserved immaculate from all stain of original sin" (Schaff, ed., *Religious Encyclopedia*, vol. 2, p. 1064).

[12] Critical historians do this. They use various historical criteria to deny that such and such a saying of Jesus was really said by him, or that such and such a miracle was really done by him. But none of these historians claims that they are retelling the story of the incarnate Word *because of the inspiration of the Spirit*. In other words, my point here is not that there are no attacks on the historical Jesus, but that the role of the Spirit is not to replace the role of the book, and that the true incarnate Word is not revealed by the Spirit apart from the external Word.

to reveal the incarnate Word, Jesus Christ, to all succeeding generations *through a book*, especially the Gospels. Luther put it like this:

> The apostles themselves considered it necessary to put the
> New Testament into Greek and to bind it fast to that lan-
> guage, doubtless in order to preserve it for us safe and
> sound as in a sacred ark. For they foresaw all that was to
> come and now has come to pass, and knew that if it were
> contained only in one's head, wild and fearful disorder and
> confusion, and many various interpretations, fancies and
> doctrines would arise in the Church, which could be pre-
> vented and from which the plain man could be protected
> only by committing the New Testament to writing and
> language.[13]

The ministry of the internal Spirit does not nullify the ministry
of the "external Word." The Spirit does not duplicate what the
book was designed to do. The Spirit glorifies the incarnate Word
of the Gospels, but he does not re-narrate his words and deeds
for illiterate people or negligent pastors.

The immense implication of this for the pastoral ministry
and lay ministry is that *ministers are essentially brokers of the
Word of God transmitted in a book*. We are fundamentally readers and teachers and proclaimers of the message of the book.
And all of this is for the glory of the incarnate Word and by the
power of the indwelling Spirit. But neither the indwelling Spirit
nor the incarnate Word leads us away from the book that Luther
called "the external Word." Christ stands forth for our *worship* and our *fellowship* and our *obedience* from the "external
Word." This is where we see "the glory of God in the face of

---

[13] Hugh T. Kerr, *A Compend of Luther's Theology* (Philadelphia: The Westminster Press, 1943),
p. 17.

Christ" (2 Corinthians 4:6). So it is for the sake of Christ that the Spirit broods over the book where Christ is clear, not over trances where he is obscure.

What difference did this discovery of the book make in the way Luther carried out his ministry of the Word? What can we learn from Luther at study? His entire professional life was lived as a professor in the University of Wittenberg. So it will be helpful to trace his life up to that point and then ask why a professor can be a helpful model for pastors and laypeople who care about the "external Word" of God.

The Pathway to the Professorship

Luther was born November 10, 1483, in Eisleben, Germany, to a copper miner. His father had wanted him to enter the legal profession. So he studied at the University on the way to that vocation. According to Heiko Oberman, "There is hardly any authenticated information about those first eighteen years which led Luther to the threshold of the University of Erfurt."[14]

In 1502, at the age of nineteen he received his Bachelor's degree, ranking, unimpressively, thirtieth of fifty-seven in his class. In January 1505, he received his Master of Arts at Erfurt and ranked second among seventeen candidates. That summer, the providential Damascus-like experience happened. On July 2, on the way home from law school, he was caught in a thunderstorm and was hurled to the ground by lightning. He cried out, "Help me, St. Anne; I will become a monk."[15] He feared for his soul

---

[14] Oberman, *Luther: Man Between God and the Devil*, p. 102.
[15] Ibid., p. 92.

and did not know how to find safety in the Gospel. So he took the next best thing, the monastery.

Fifteen days later, to his father's dismay, he kept his vow. On July 17, 1505, he knocked at the gate of the Augustinian Hermits in Erfurt and asked the prior to accept him into the order. Later he said this choice was a flagrant sin—"not worth a farthing" because made against his father and out of fear. Then he added, "But how much good the merciful Lord has allowed to come of it!"[16] We see this kind of merciful providence over and over again in the history of the church. We saw it powerfully in the life of Augustine, and we will see it in Calvin's life too. It should protect us from the paralyzing effects of bad decisions in our past. God is not hindered in his sovereign designs from leading us, as he did Luther, out of blunders into fruitful lives of joy.

Luther was twenty-one years old when he became an Augustinian monk. It would be twenty years before he married Katharina von Bora on June 13, 1525. So there were twenty more years of wrestling with the temptations of a single man who had very powerful drives. But "in the monastery," he said, "I did not think about women, money, or possessions; instead my heart trembled and fidgeted about whether God would bestow His grace on me. . . . For I had strayed from faith and could not but imagine that I had angered God, whom I in turn had to appease by doing good works."[17] There was no theological gamesmanship in Luther's early studies. He said, "If I could believe that God was not angry with me, I would stand on my head for joy."[18]

---

[16] Ibid., p. 125.
[17] Ibid., p. 128.
[18] Ibid., p. 315. Which is why, when he found the gospel, he was able to turn the world upside-down.

On Easter, April 3, 1507, he was ordained to the priesthood, and on May 2 he celebrated his first mass. He was so overwhelmed at the thought of God's majesty, he says, that he almost ran away. The prior persuaded him to continue. Oberman says that this incident of fear and trembling was not isolated in Luther's life.

> A sense of the *mysterium tremendum*, of the holiness of God, was to be characteristic of Luther throughout his life. It prevented pious routine from creeping into his relations with God and kept his Bible studies, prayers, or reading of the mass from declining into a mechanical matter of course: his ultimate concern in all these is the encounter with the living God.[19]

For two years Luther taught aspects of philosophy to the younger monks. He said later that teaching philosophy was like waiting for the real thing.[20] In 1509, the real thing came when his beloved superior and counselor and friend, Johannes von Staupitz, "admitted Luther to the Bible." That is, he allowed Luther to teach Bible instead of moral philosophy—Paul instead of Aristotle. Three years later on October 19, 1512, at the age of twenty-eight Luther received his Doctor's degree in theology, and Staupitz turned over to him the chair in Biblical Theology at the University of Wittenberg, which Luther held the rest of his life.

So Luther was a university theology professor all his professional life. This causes us to raise the question whether he can really serve as any kind of model for the rest of us who are not professors. Can he really understand, for example, what those of us who are pastors face in our kind of ministry? But it would be

[19] Ibid., p. 137.
[20] Ibid., p. 145.

a mistake to think Luther has nothing to show us. At least three things unite him to us who are pastors—and thus all the closer to the people in the pew.

Why Pastors (and Others) Should Listen to Luther

First, he was a preacher—more a preacher than most pastors. He knew the burden and the pressure of weekly preaching. There were two churches in Wittenberg, the town church and the castle church. Luther was a regular preacher at the town church. He said, "If I could today become king or emperor, I would not give up my office as preacher."[21] He was driven by a passion for the exaltation of God in the Word. In one of his prayers he says, "Dear Lord God, I want to preach so that you are glorified. I want to speak of you, praise you, praise your name. Although I probably cannot make it turn out well, won't you make it turn out well?"[22]

To feel the force of this commitment you have to realize that in the church in Wittenberg there were no church programs, but only worship and preaching. On Sundays there were the 5:00 A.M. worship with a sermon on the Epistle, the 10:00 A.M. service with a sermon on the Gospel, and an afternoon message on the Old Testament or catechism. Monday and Tuesday sermons were on the Catechism; Wednesdays on Matthew; Thursdays and Fridays on the Apostolic letters; and Saturday on John.[23]

Luther was not the pastor of the town church. His friend, Johannes Bugenhagen, was pastor there from 1521 to 1558. But

---

[21] Fred W. Meuser, *Luther the Preacher* (Minneapolis: Augsburg Publishing House, 1983), p. 39.
[22] Ibid., p. 51.
[23] Ibid., pp. 37-38.

Luther shared the preaching virtually every week he was in town. He preached because the people of the town wanted to hear him and because he and his contemporaries understood his doctorate in theology to be a call to teach the Word of God to the whole church. So Luther would often preach twice on Sunday and once during the week. Walther von Loewenich said in his biography, "Luther was one of the greatest preachers in the history of Christendom. . . . Between 1510 and 1546 Luther preached approximately 3000 sermons. Frequently he preached several times a week, often two or more times a day."[24]

For example, he preached 117 sermons in Wittenberg in 1522 and 137 sermons the next year. In 1528 he preached almost 200 times, and from 1529 we have 121 sermons. So the average in those four years was one sermon every two and a half days. As Fred Meuser says in his book on Luther's preaching, "Never a weekend off—he knows all about that. Never even a weekday off. Never any respite at all from preaching, teaching, private study, production, writing, counseling."[25] That's his first link with those of us who are pastors. He knows the burden of preaching.

Second, like most pastors, Luther was a family man. At least from age forty-one to his death at sixty-two. He knew the pressure and the heartache of having and rearing and losing children. Katie bore him six children in quick succession: Johannes (1526), Elisabeth (1527), Magdalena (1529), Martin (1531), Paul (1533), and Margaret (1534). Do a little computing here. The year between Elisabeth and Magdalena was the year he preached 200 times

---

[24] Walther von Loewenich, *Luther: The Man and His Work*, trans. Lawrence W. Denef (Minneapolis: Augsburg Publishing House, 1986, orig. 1982), p. 353.
[25] Meuser, *Luther the Preacher*, p. 27.

(more than once every other day). Add to this that Elisabeth died that year at eight months old, but he kept on going under that pain.

And lest we think Luther neglected the children, consider that on Sunday afternoons, often after preaching twice, Luther led the household devotions, which were virtually another worship service for an hour, including the guests as well as the children.[26] So Luther knew the pressures of being a public and family man.

Third, Luther was a churchman, not an ivory-tower theological scholar. He was not only part of almost all the controversies and conferences of his day, he was usually the leader. There was the Heidelberg Disputation (1518), the encounter with Cardinal Cajetan at Augsburg (1518), the Leipzig Disputation with Johann Eck and Andrew Karlstadt (1519), the Diet of Worms before the Emperor (1521), the Marburg Colloquy with Zwingli (1529), and the Diet of Augsburg (though he was not there in person, 1530).

Besides active personal involvement in church conferences, there was the unbelievable stream of publications that are all related to the guidance of the church. For example, in 1520 he wrote 133 works; in 1522, 130; in 1523, 183 (one every other day!), and just as many in 1524.[27] He was the lightning rod for every criticism against the Reformation. "All flocked to him, besieging his door hourly, trooped citizens, doctors, princes. Diplomatic enigmas were to be solved, knotty theological points were to be settled, the ethics of social life were to be laid down."[28]

With the breakdown of the medieval system of church life, a whole new way of thinking about church and the Christian life

---

[26] Ibid., p. 38.
[27] W. Carlos Martyn, *The Life and Times of Martin Luther* (New York: American Tract Society, 1866), p. 473.
[28] Ibid., p. 272.

had to be developed. And in Germany that task fell in large measure to Martin Luther. It is astonishing how he threw himself into the mundane matters of parish life. For example, when it was decided that "Visitors" from the state and university would be sent to each parish to assess the condition of the church and make suggestions for church life, Luther took it upon himself to write the guidelines: "Instructions for the Visitors of Parish Pastors in Electoral Saxony." He addressed a broad array of practical issues. When he came to the education of children, he went so far as to dictate how the lower grades should be divided into three groups: pre-readers, readers, and advanced readers. Then he made suggestions for teaching them.

> They shall first learn to read the primer in which are found the alphabet, the Lord's prayer, the Creed, and other prayers. When they have learned this they shall be given Donatus and Cato, to read Donatus and to expound Cato. The schoolmaster is to expound one or two verses at a time, and the children are to repeat these at a later time, so that they thereby build up a vocabulary.[29]

We see then that this university professor was intensely involved in trying to solve the most practical ministry problems from the cradle to the grave. He did not do his studying in the uninterrupted leisure of sabbaticals and long summers. He was constantly besieged and constantly at work.

So, though he was a university professor, there is good reason for pastors and lay ministers of the Word to look at his work

---

[29] Conrad Bergendoff, ed., *Church and Ministry II,* vol. 40, *Luther's Works* (Philadelphia: Muhlenberg Press, 1958), pp. 315-316.

and listen to his words, in order to learn and be inspired for the ministry of the Word—the "external Word," the book.

Luther at Study: The Difference the Book Made

For Luther, the importance of study was so interwoven with his discovery of the true Gospel that he could never treat study as anything other than utterly crucial and life-giving and history-shaping. Study had been his gateway to the gospel and to the Reformation and to God. We take so much for granted today about the truth and about the Word that we can hardly imagine what it cost Luther to break through to the truth, and to sustain access to the Word. Study mattered. His life and the life of the church hung on it. We need to ask whether all the ground gained by Luther and the other Reformers may be lost over time if we lose this passion for study, while assuming that truth will remain obvious and available.

To see this intertwining of study and the rediscovery of the Gospel, let's go back to the early years in Wittenberg. Luther dates his discovery of the Gospel in 1518 during a series of lectures on Psalms.[30] He tells the story in his *Preface to the Complete Edition of Luther's Latin Writings*. This account of the discovery is taken from that Preface, written on March 5, 1545, the year before his death. Watch for the references to his study of Scripture (with emphasis added).

> *I had indeed been captivated with an extraordinary ardor for understanding Paul in the Epistle to the Romans.* But

---

[30] John Dillenberger, ed., *Martin Luther: Selections from His Writings* (Garden City, NY: Doubleday and Co., 1961), p. xvii.

up till then it was . . . a single word in Chapter 1 [v. 17], "In it the righteousness of God is revealed," that had stood in my way. For I hated that word "righteousness of God," which *according to the use and custom of all the teachers, I had been taught to understand philosophically* regarding the formal or active righteousness, as they called it, with which God is righteous and punishes the unrighteous sinner.

Though I lived as a monk without reproach, I felt that I was a sinner before God with an extremely disturbed conscience. I could not believe that he was placated by my satisfaction. I did not love, yes, I hated the righteous God who punishes sinners, and secretly, if not blasphemously, certainly murmuring greatly, I was angry with God, and said, "As if, indeed, it is not enough, that miserable sinners, eternally lost through original sin, are crushed by every kind of calamity by the law of the decalogue, without having God add pain to pain by the gospel and also by the gospel threatening us with his righteous wrath!" Thus I raged with a fierce and troubled conscience. Nevertheless, *I beat importunately upon Paul at that place, most ardently desiring to know what St. Paul wanted.*

At last, by the mercy of God, *meditating day and night,* I gave heed to the context of the words, namely, "In it the righteousness of God is revealed, as it is written, 'He who through faith is righteous shall live.'" There *I began to understand* [that] the righteousness of God is that by which the righteous lives by a gift of God, namely by faith. And this is the meaning: the righteousness of God is revealed by the gospel, namely, the passive righteousness with which [the] merciful God justifies us by faith, as it is written, "He who through faith is righteous shall live." Here I felt that I was altogether born again and had entered paradise itself through open gates. Here a totally other face of the entire Scripture showed itself to me. *Thereupon I ran through the Scriptures from memory. . . .*

And I extolled my sweetest word with a love as great as the hatred with which I had before hated the word "righteousness of God." Thus *that place in Paul* was for me truly the gate to paradise.[31]

Notice how God was bringing Luther to the light of the Gospel of justification. Six sentences—all of them revealing the intensity of study and wrestling with the biblical text:

I had indeed been captivated with an *extraordinary ardor* for understanding Paul in the Epistle to the Romans.

According to the use and custom of all the teachers, I had been taught to understand *philosophically* [an approach to study from which he was breaking free].

I beat importunately upon Paul at that place, most ardently desiring to know what St. Paul wanted.

At last, by the mercy of God, *meditating day and night*, I gave heed to the context of the words.

Thereupon I ran through *the Scriptures from memory*.

That place in Paul was for me truly the gate to paradise.

The seeds of all Luther's study habits are there or are clearly implied. What was it, then, that marked the man Luther at study and yielded such history-shaping discoveries?

---

[31] Ibid., pp. 11-12.

1. *Luther came to elevate the biblical text itself far above the teachings of commentators or church fathers.*

This was not the conclusion of laziness. Melanchthon, Luther's friend and colleague at Wittenberg, said Luther knew his dogmatics so well in the early days that he could quote whole pages of Gabriel Biel (the standard dogmatics text, published 1488) by heart.[32] It wasn't lack of energy for the fathers and the philosophers that limited his focus; it was an overriding passion for the superiority of the biblical text itself.

He wrote in 1533, "For a number of years I have now annually read through the Bible twice. If the Bible were a large, mighty tree and all its words were little branches, I have tapped at all the branches, eager to know what was there and what it had to offer."[33] Oberman says Luther kept to that practice for at least ten years.[34] The Bible had come to mean more to Luther than all the fathers and commentators.

"He who is well acquainted with the text of Scripture," Luther said in 1538, "is a distinguished theologian. For a Bible passage or text is of more value than the comments of four authors."[35] In his *Open Letter to the Christian Nobility,* Luther explained his concern:

> The writings of all the holy fathers should be read only for a time, in order that through them we may be led to the Holy Scriptures. As it is, however, we read them only to be absorbed in them and never come to the Scriptures. We are like men who study the signposts and never travel

---

[32] Oberman, *Luther: Man Between God and the Devil,* p. 138.
[33] Plass, *What Luther Says,* vol. 1, p. 83.
[34] Oberman, *Luther: Man Between God and the Devil,* p. 173.
[35] Plass, *What Luther Says,* vol. 3, p. 1355.

the road. The dear fathers wished by their writing, to lead us to the Scriptures, but we so use them as to be led away from the Scriptures, though the Scriptures alone are our vineyard in which we ought all to work and toil.[36]

The Bible is the pastor's vineyard, where he ought to work and toil. But, Luther complained in 1539, "The Bible is being buried by the wealth of commentaries, and the text is being neglected, although in every branch of learning they are the best who are well acquainted with the text."[37] This is no mere purist or classicist allegiance to the sources. This is the testimony of a man who found life at the original *spring* in the mountain, not the secondary *stream* in the valley. It was a matter of life and death whether one studied the text of Scripture itself or spent most of his time reading commentaries and secondary literature. Looking back on the early days of his study of the Scriptures, Luther said,

> When I was young, I read the Bible over and over and over again, and was so perfectly acquainted with it, that I could, in an instant, have pointed to any verse that might have been mentioned. I then read the commentators, but I soon threw them aside, for I found therein many things my conscience could not approve, as being contrary to the sacred text. 'Tis always better to see with one's own eyes than with those of other people.[38]

Luther doesn't mean in all this that there is no place at all for reading other books. After all, he wrote books. But he counsels us to make them secondary and make them few. He says,

---

[36] Kerr, *A Compend of Luther's Theology*, p. 13.
[37] Plass, *What Luther Says*, vol. 1, p. 97.
[38] Kerr, *A Compend of Luther's Theology*, p. 16.

A student who does not want his labor wasted must so read and reread some good writer that the author is changed, as it were, into his flesh and blood. For a great variety of reading confuses and does not teach. It makes the student like a man who dwells everywhere and, therefore, nowhere in particular. Just as we do not daily enjoy the society of every one of our friends but only that of a chosen few, so it should also be in our studying.[39]

The number of theological books should . . . be reduced, and a selection should be made of the best of them; for many books do not make men learned, nor does much reading. But reading something good, and reading it frequently, however little it may be, is the practice that makes men learned in the Scripture and makes them pious besides.[40]

2. *This radical focus on the text of Scripture itself with secondary literature in secondary place leads Luther to an intense and serious grappling with the very words of Paul and the other biblical writers.*

That's the second characteristic of Luther at study. Instead of running to the commentaries and fathers, he says, "*I beat importunately upon Paul* at that place, most ardently desiring to know what St. Paul wanted." This was not an isolated incident, but a habit.

He told his students that the exegete should treat a difficult passage no differently than Moses did the rock in the desert, which he smote with his rod until water gushed out for his thirsty people.[41] In other words, strike the text. "I beat importunately upon

[39] Plass, *What Luther Says,* vol. 1, p. 112.
[40] Ibid., p. 113.
[41] Oberman, *Luther: Man Between God and the Devil,* p. 224.

Paul." There is a great incentive in this beating on the text: "The Bible is a remarkable fountain: the more one draws and drinks of it, the more it stimulates thirst."[42]

In the summer and fall of 1526, Luther took up the challenge to lecture on Ecclesiastes to the small band of students who stayed behind in Wittenberg during a plague that was threatening the city. "Solomon the preacher," he wrote to a friend, "is giving me a hard time, as though he begrudged anyone lecturing on him. But he must yield."[43]

That is what study was to Luther—taking a text the way Jacob took the angel of the Lord, and saying: "It must yield. I *will* hear and know the Word of God in this text for my soul and for the church!" That's how he broke through to the meaning of "the righteousness of God" in justification. And that is how he broke through tradition and philosophy again and again.

3. *The power and preciousness of what Luther saw when he beat importunately upon Paul's language convinced him forever that reading Greek and Hebrew was one of the greatest privileges and responsibilities of the Reformation preacher.*

Again the motive and conviction here are not academic commitments to high-level scholarship, but spiritual commitments to proclaiming and preserving a pure Gospel.

Luther spoke against the backdrop of a thousand years of church darkness without the Word when he said boldly, "It is certain that unless the languages [of Greek and Hebrew] remain, the Gospel must finally perish."[44] He asks, "Do you inquire what use

---

[42] Plass, *What Luther Says*, vol. 1, p. 67.
[43] Heinrich Bornkamm, trans. E. Theodore Bachmann, *Luther in Mid-Career, 1521-1530* (Philadelphia: Fortress Press, 1983, orig. 1979), p. 564.
[44] Kerr, *A Compend of Luther's Theology*, p. 17.

there is in learning the languages? . . . Do you say, 'We can read the Bible very well in German?'" (As many American pastors today say, "Isn't a good English translation sufficient?") Luther answers,

> Without languages we could not have received the gospel. Languages are the scabbard that contains the sword of the Spirit; they are the [case] which contains the priceless jewels of antique thought; they are the vessel that holds the wine; and as the gospel says, they are the baskets in which the loaves and fishes are kept to feed the multitude.
>
> If we neglect the literature we shall eventually lose the gospel. . . . No sooner did men cease to cultivate the languages than Christendom declined, even until it fell under the undisputed dominion of the pope. But no sooner was this torch relighted, than this papal owl fled with a shriek into congenial gloom. . . . In former times the fathers were frequently mistaken, because they were ignorant of the languages and in our days there are some who, like the Waldenses, do not think the languages of any use; but although their doctrine is good, they have often erred in the real meaning of the sacred text; they are without arms against error, and I fear much that their faith will not remain pure.[45]

The main issue was the preservation and the purity of the faith. Where the languages are not prized and pursued, care in bib-

---

[45] Martyn, *The Life and Times of Martin Luther*, pp. 474-475. Luther did not praise Augustine in this regard, but would have occasion to call him to account for his weakness in Greek and his virtual ignorance of Hebrew (Peter Brown, *Augustine of Hippo* [Berkeley, CA: University of California Press, 1969], p. 257). Augustine's bent toward allegorizing would have to be corrected by those who attended more closely to the text and its meaning in the original languages. Augustine learned Greek superficially as a child, but disliked it intensely ("Even now I cannot fully understand why the Greek language, which I learned as a child, was so distasteful to me. I loved Latin," Augustine, *Confessions*, trans. R. S. Pine-Coffin [New York: Penguin Books, 1961], p. 33, [I, 13]) and never was able to use it with great facility. "Only a few times when confronted with Julian of Eclanum, the Pelagian, would Augustine try to refute his critics by comparing the original Greek with translations" (Brown, *Augustine of Hippo*, p. 171). Let the remarkable achievement of Augustine encourage those who do not have the privilege of studying the original languages. But let us beware of making the compensating power of his extraordinary abilities an excuse for not improving ours with the gift of Greek and Hebrew.

lical observation and biblical thinking and concern for truth decreases. It has to, because the tools to think otherwise are not present. This was an intensely real possibility for Luther because he had known it. He said, "If the languages had not made me positive as to the true meaning of the word, I might have still remained a chained monk, engaged in quietly preaching Romish errors in the obscurity of a cloister; the pope, the sophists, and their antichristian empire would have remained unshaken."[46] In other words, he attributes the breakthrough of the Reformation to the penetrating power of the original languages.

The great linguistic event of Luther's time was the appearance of the Greek New Testament edited by Desiderius Erasmus. As soon as it appeared in the middle of the summer session of 1516, Luther obtained a copy and began to study it and use it in his lectures on Romans 9. He did this even though Erasmus was a theological adversary. Having the languages was such a treasure to Luther, he would have gone to school with the devil in order to learn them—as he might have said it.

He was convinced that many impediments in study would be found without the help of the languages. "St. Augustine," he said, "is compelled to confess, when he writes in *De Doctrina Christiana*, that a Christian teacher who is to expound Scripture has need also of the Greek and the Hebrew languages in addition to the Latin; otherwise it is impossible for him not to run into obstacles everywhere."[47]

And he was persuaded that knowing the languages would bring freshness and force to preaching. He said,

[46] Martyn, *The Life and Times of Martin Luther*, p. 474.
[47] Plass, *What Luther Says,* vol. 1, p. 95. But see note 45.

Though the faith and the Gospel may be proclaimed by simple preachers without the languages, such preaching is flat and tame, men grow at last wearied and disgusted and it falls to the ground. But when the preacher is versed in the languages, his discourse has freshness and force, the whole of Scripture is treated, and faith finds itself constantly renewed by a continual variety of words and works.[48]

Now that is a discouraging overstatement for many pastors who never studied or have lost their Greek and Hebrew. What I would say is that knowing the languages can make any devoted preacher a better preacher—more fresh, more faithful, more confident, more penetrating. But it is possible to preach faithfully without them—at least for a season, while pastors stand on the previous generations of expositors who knew and used the languages. The test of our faithfulness to the Word, if we cannot read the languages, is this: Do we have a large enough concern for the church of Jesus Christ to promote their preservation and their widespread teaching and use in the churches? Or do we, out of self-protection, minimize their importance because to do otherwise stings too badly?

It may be that for many of us today Luther's strong words about our neglect and indifference are accurate when he says,

It is a sin and shame not to know our own book or to understand the speech and words of our God; it is a still greater sin and loss that we do not study languages, especially in these days when God is offering and giving us men and books and every facility and inducement to this study,

---

[48] Kerr, *A Compend of Luther's Theology,* p. 148.

and desires his Bible to be an open book. O how happy the dear fathers would have been if they had our opportunity to study the languages and come thus prepared to the Holy Scriptures! What great toil and effort it cost them to gather up a few crumbs, while we with half the labor— yes, almost without any labor at all—can acquire the whole loaf! O how their effort puts our indolence to shame![49]

4. *This reference to "indolence" leads us to the fourth characteristic of Luther at study, namely, extraordinary diligence in spite of tremendous obstacles.*

What he accomplished borders on the superhuman, and of course makes pygmies of us all.

His job as professor of Bible at the University of Wittenberg was full-time work of its own. He wrote theological treatises by the score: biblical, homiletical, liturgical, educational, devotional, and political, some of which have shaped Protestant church life for centuries. All the while he was translating the whole of the Scriptures into German, a language that he helped to shape by that very translation. He carried on a voluminous correspondence, for he was constantly asked for advice and counsel. Travel, meetings, conferences, and colloquies were the order of the day. All the while he was preaching regularly to a congregation that he must have regarded as a showcase of the Reformation.[50]

We are not Luther and could never be, no matter how hard we tried. But the point here is: Do we work at our studies with rigor

---

[49] Meuser, *Luther the Preacher*, p. 43. With computer programs for instruction and use of the languages, how much more true is this today than when it was written!
[50] Ibid., p. 27.

and diligence or are we slothful and casual about it, as if nothing really great is at stake?

When he was just short of sixty years old, he pleaded with pastors to be diligent and not lazy.

> Some pastors and preachers are lazy and no good. They do not pray; they do not read; they do not search the Scripture. . . . The call is: watch, study, attend to reading. In truth you cannot read too much in Scripture; and what you read you cannot read too carefully, and what you read carefully you cannot understand too well, and what you understand well you cannot teach too well, and what you teach well you cannot live too well. . . . The devil . . . the world . . . and our flesh are raging and raving against us. Therefore, dear sirs and brothers, pastors and preachers, pray, read, study, be diligent. . . . This evil, shameful time is not the season for being lazy, for sleeping and snoring.[51]

Commenting on Genesis 3:19 ("By the sweat of your face you shall eat bread"), Luther says, "The household sweat is great; the political sweat is greater; the church sweat is the greatest."[52] He responded once to those who do hard physical labor and consider the work of study a soft life:

> Sure, it would be hard for me to sit "in the saddle." But then again I would like to see the horseman who could sit still for a whole day and gaze at a book without worrying or dreaming or think about anything else. Ask . . . a preacher . . . how much work it is to speak and preach. . . . The pen is very light, that is true. . . . But in this work the

---

[51] Ibid., pp. 40-41.
[52] Plass, *What Luther Says,* vol. 2, p. 951.

best part of the human body (the head), the noblest member (the tongue), and the highest work (speech) bear the brunt of the load and work the hardest, while in other kinds of work either the hand, the foot, the back or other members do the work alone so the person can sing happily or make jokes freely which a sermon writer cannot do. Three fingers do it all . . . but the whole body and soul have to work at it.[53]

There is great danger, Luther says, in thinking we have ever gotten to a point when we fancy we don't need to study anymore. "Let ministers daily pursue their studies with diligence and constantly busy themselves with them. . . . Let them steadily keep on reading, teaching, studying, pondering, and meditating. Nor let them cease until they have discovered and are sure that they have taught the devil to death and have become more learned than God himself and all His saints"[54]—which of course means never.

Luther knew that there was such a thing as overwork and damaging, counterproductive strain. But he clearly preferred to err on the side of overwork than underwork. We see this in 1532 when he wrote, "A person should work in such a way that he remains well and does no injury to his body. We should not break our heads at work and injure our bodies. . . . I myself used to do such things, and I have racked my brains because I still have not overcome the bad habit of overworking. Nor shall I overcome it as long as I live."[55]

I don't know if the apostle Paul would have made the same

[53] Meuser, *Luther the Preacher*, pp. 44-45.
[54] Plass, *What Luther Says,* vol. 2, p. 927.
[55] Ibid., vol. 3, pp. 1496-1497.

confession at the end of his life. But he did say, "I labored even more than all of them [the other apostles]" (1 Corinthians 15:10). And in comparison to the false apostles he said, "Are they servants of Christ? (I speak as if insane) I more so; *in far more labors*, in far more imprisonments, beaten times without number, often in danger of death" (2 Corinthians 11:23). He said to the Colossians, "I labor, striving [*agōnizomenos*] according to His power, which mightily works within me" (Colossians 1:29). So it's not surprising that Luther would strive to follow his dear Paul in "far more labors."

5. Which leads us to the fifth characteristic of Luther at study, namely, suffering. For Luther, trials make a theologian. Temptation and affliction are the hermeneutical touchstones.

Luther noticed in Psalm 119 that the psalmist not only prayed and meditated over the Word of God in order to understand it; he also suffered in order to understand it. Psalm 119:67, 71 says, "Before I was afflicted I went astray, but now I keep Your word. . . . It is good for me that I was afflicted, that I may learn Your statutes." An indispensable key to understanding the Scriptures is suffering in the path of righteousness.

Thus Luther said : "I want you to know how to study theology in the right way. I have practiced this method myself. . . . Here you will find three rules. They are frequently proposed throughout Psalm [119] and run thus: *Oratio, meditatio, tentatio* (prayer, meditation, tribulation)."[56] And tribulation (*Anfechtungen*) he called the "touchstone." "[These rules] teach you not only to know and understand, but also to experience

---

[56] Ibid., p. 1359.

how right, how true, how sweet, how lovely, how mighty, how comforting God's word is: it is wisdom supreme."[57]

He proved the value of trials over and over again in his own experience. "For as soon as God's Word becomes known through you," he says, "the devil will afflict you, will make a real [theological] doctor of you, and will teach you by his temptations to seek and to love God's Word. For I myself . . . owe my papists many thanks for so beating, pressing, and frightening me through the devil's raging that they have turned me into a fairly good theologian, driving me to a goal I should never have reached."[58]

Suffering was woven into life for Luther. Keep in mind that from 1521 on, Luther lived under the ban of the empire. Emperor Charles V said, "I have decided to mobilize everything against Luther: my kingdoms and dominions, my friends, my body, my blood and my soul."[59] He could be legally killed, except where he was protected by his prince, Frederick of Saxony.

He endured relentless slander of the most cruel kind. He once observed, "If the Devil can do nothing against the teachings, he attacks the person, lying, slandering, cursing, and ranting at him. Just as the papists' Beelzebub did to me when he could not subdue my Gospel, he wrote that I was possessed by the Devil, was a changeling, my beloved mother a whore and bath attendant."[60]

Physically he suffered from excruciating kidney stones and headaches, with buzzing in his ears and ear infections and incapacitating constipation and hemorrhoids. "I nearly gave up the

---

[57] Ibid., p. 1360.
[58] Ibid.
[59] Oberman, *Luther: Man Between God and the Devil*, p. 29.
[60] Ibid., p. 88.

ghost—and now, bathed in blood, can find no peace. What took four days to heal immediately tears open again."[61]

It's not surprising then that emotionally and spiritually he would undergo the most horrible struggles. For example, in a letter to Melanchthon on August 2, 1527, he writes, "For more than a week I have been thrown back and forth in death and Hell; my whole body feels beaten, my limbs are still trembling. I almost lost Christ completely, driven about on the waves and storms of despair and blasphemy against God. But because of the intercession of the faithful, God began to take mercy on me and tore my soul from the depths of Hell."[62]

On the outside, to many, he looked invulnerable. But those close to him knew the *tentatio*. Again he wrote to Melanchthon from the Wartburg castle on July 13, 1521, while he was supposedly working feverishly on the translation of the New Testament:

> I sit here at ease, hardened and unfeeling—alas! praying little, grieving little for the Church of God, burning rather in the fierce fires of my untamed flesh. It comes to this: I *should* be afire in the spirit; in reality I am afire in the flesh, with lust, laziness, idleness, sleepiness. It is perhaps because you have all ceased praying for me that God has turned away from me. . . . For the last eight days I have written nothing, nor prayed nor studied, partly from self-indulgence, partly from another vexatious handicap [constipation and piles]. . . . I really cannot stand it any longer. . . . Pray for me, I beg you, for in my seclusion here I am submerged in sins.[63]

---

[61] Ibid., p. 328.
[62] Ibid., p. 323.
[63] E. G. Rupp and Benjamin Drewery, eds., *Martin Luther: Documents of Modern History* (New York: St. Martin's Press, 1970), pp. 72-73.

These were the trials that he said made him a theologian. These experiences were as much a part of his exegetical labors as were his Greek lexicon. This should cause us to think twice before we begrudge the trials of our ministry. How often I am tempted to think that the pressures and conflicts and frustrations are simply distractions from the business of study and understanding. Luther (and Psalm 119:71) teach us to see it all another way. That stressful visit that interrupted your study may well be the very lens through which the text will open to you as never before. *Tentatio*—trial, the thorn in the flesh—is Satan's unwitting contribution to our becoming good theologians.

The triumph in these trials is not our own doing. We are utterly dependent on God's free grace to supply our strength and restore our faith. Luther confessed that in his sense of abandonment and torment, faith "exceeds my powers."[64] Here we must cry out to God alone.

6. *Which leads to the final characteristic of Luther at study: prayer and reverent dependence on the all-sufficiency of God. And here the theology and methodology of Luther become almost identical.*

In typical paradoxical form, Luther seems to take back almost everything he has said about study when he writes in 1518,

> That the Holy Scriptures cannot be penetrated by study and talent is most certain. Therefore your first duty is to begin to pray, and to pray to this effect that if it please God to accomplish something for His glory—not for yours or any other person's—He may very graciously grant you a true understanding of His words. For no master of the

---

[64] Oberman, *Luther: Man Between God and the Devil*, p. 323.

divine words exists except the Author of these words, as He says: "They shall be all taught of God" (John 6:45). You must, therefore, completely despair of your own industry and ability and rely solely on the inspiration of the Spirit.[65]

Luther does not mean that we should leave the "external Word" in mystical reverie, but that we should bathe all our work in prayer, and cast ourselves so wholly on God that he enters and sustains and prospers all our study.

Since the Holy Writ wants to be dealt with in fear and humility and penetrated more by studying [!] with pious prayer than with keenness of intellect, therefore it is impossible for those who rely only on their intellect and rush into Scripture with dirty feet, like pigs, as though Scripture were merely a sort of human knowledge, not to harm themselves and others whom they instruct.[66]

Again he sees the psalmist in Psalm 119 not only suffering and meditating, but praying again and again:

Psalm 119:18, "Open my eyes, that I may behold wonderful things from Your law." Psalm 119:27, "Make me understand the way of Your precepts." Psalm 119:34, "Give me understanding, that I may observe Your law." Psalm 119:35-37, "Make me walk in the path of Your commandments, for I delight in it. Incline my heart to Your testimonies, and not to gain. And revive me in Your ways."

So he concludes that the true biblical way to study the Bible

---

[65] Plass, *What Luther Says*, vol. 1, p. 77.
[66] Ibid., vol. 1, p. 78.

will be saturated with prayer and self-doubt and God-reliance moment by moment:

> You should completely despair of your own sense and reason, for by these you will not attain the goal. . . . Rather kneel down in your private little room and with sincere humility and earnestness pray God, through His dear Son, graciously to grant you His Holy Spirit to enlighten and guide you and give you understanding.[67]

Luther's emphasis on prayer in study is rooted in his theology, and here is where his methodology and his theology become one. He was persuaded from Romans 8:7 and elsewhere that "the natural mind cannot do anything godly. It does not perceive the wrath of God, therefore cannot rightly fear him. It does not see the goodness of God, therefore cannot trust or believe in him either. Therefore we should constantly pray that God will bring forth his gifts in us."[68] All our study is futile without the work of God overcoming our blindness and hardheartedness.

Luther and Augustine were one on this central issue of the Reformation. At the heart of Luther's theology was a total dependence on the freedom of God's omnipotent grace rescuing powerless man from the bondage of the will. Concerning free will Luther said, "Man has in his own power a freedom of the will to do or not to do external works, regulated by law and punishment. . . . On the other hand, man cannot by his own power purify his heart and bring forth godly gifts, such as true repentance or sins, a true, as over against an artificial, fear of God, true faith, sin-

---

[67] Ibid., vol. 3, p. 1359.
[68] Bergendoff, ed., *Church and Ministry II*, vol. 40, *Luther's Works*, p. 302.

cere love, chastity. . . ."[69] In other words, the will is "free" to move our action, but beneath the will there is a bondage that can only be overcome by the free grace of God. Luther saw this bondage of the will as the root issue in the fight with Rome and its most discerning spokesman, Erasmus.

Luther's book by that name, *The Bondage of the Will*, published in 1525, was an answer to Erasmus' book, *The Freedom of the Will*. Luther regarded this one book of his—*The Bondage of the Will*—as his "best theological book, and the only one in that class worthy of publication."[70]

To understand Luther's theology and his methodology of study, it is extremely important to recognize that he conceded that Erasmus, more than any other opponent, had realized that the powerlessness of man before God, not the indulgence controversy or purgatory, was the central question of the Christian faith. Man is powerless to justify himself, powerless to sanctify himself, powerless to study as he ought, and powerless to trust God to do anything about this. He had seen this in Paul, and it was confirmed in the great battles between Augustine and Pelagius.

Erasmus' exaltation of man's will as free to overcome its own sin and bondage was, in Luther's mind, an assault on the freedom of God's grace and therefore an attack on the very Gospel itself. In Luther's summary of faith in 1528 he wrote,

> I condemn and reject as nothing but error all doctrines which exalt our "free will" as being directly opposed to this mediation and grace of our Lord Jesus Christ. For since, apart from Christ, sin and death are our masters and

---

[69] Ibid., vol. 40, *Luther's Works*, p. 301.
[70] Dillenberger, ed., *Martin Luther: Selections from His Writings*, p. 167.

the devil is our god and prince, there can be no strength or power, no wit or wisdom, by which we can fit or fashion ourselves for righteousness and life. On the contrary, blinded and captivated, we are bound to be the subjects of Satan and sin, doing and thinking what pleases him and is opposed to God and His commandments.[71]

Luther realized that the issue of man's bondage to sin and his moral inability to believe or make himself right—including the inability to study rightly—was the root issue of the Reformation. The freedom of God, and therefore the freedom of the Gospel and therefore the glory of God and the salvation of men, were at stake in this controversy. Therefore Luther loved the message of *The Bondage of the Will*, ascribing all freedom and power and grace to God, and all powerlessness and dependency to man.

In his explanation of Galatians 1:11-12, he recounted:

I recall that at the beginning of my cause Dr. Staupitz . . . said to me: It pleases me that the doctrine which you preach ascribes the glory and everything to God alone and nothing to man; for to God (that is clearer than the sun) one cannot ascribe too much glory, goodness, etc. This word comforted and strengthened me greatly at the time. And it is true that the doctrine of the Gospel takes all glory, wisdom, righteousness, etc., from men and ascribes them to the Creator alone, who makes everything out of nothing.[72]

This is why prayer is the root of Luther's approach to studying God's Word. Prayer is the echo of the freedom and sufficiency

---

[71] Plass, *What Luther Says*, vol. 3, pp. 1376-1377.
[72] Ibid., vol. 3, p. 1374.

of God in the heart of powerless man. It is the way Luther conceived of his theology and the way he pursued his studies. And it is the way he died.

At 3:00 A.M. on February 18, 1546, Luther died. His last recorded words were, "*Wir sein Bettler. Hoc est verum.*" "We are beggars. This is true."[73] God is free—utterly free—in his grace. And we are beggars—pray-ers. That is how we live, that is how we die, and that is how we study, so that God gets the glory and we get the grace.

---

[73] Oberman, *Luther: Man Between God and the Devil*, p. 324.

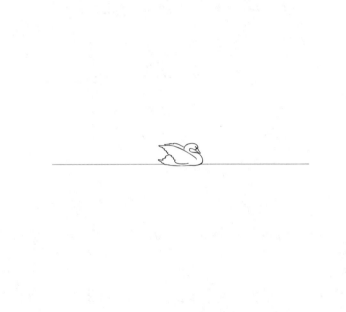

Let the pastors boldly dare all things by the word of God. . . .

Let them constrain

all the power, glory, and excellence of the world

to give place to and to obey the divine majesty of this word.

Let them enjoin everyone by it,

from the highest to the lowest.

Let them edify the body of Christ.

Let them devastate Satan's reign.

Let them pasture the sheep,

kill the wolves,

instruct and exhort the rebellious.

Let them bind and loose thunder and lightning,

if necessary,

but let them do all according to the word of God.

JOHN CALVIN

SERMONS ON THE EPISTLE TO THE EPHESIANS

3

THE DIVINE MAJESTY OF THE WORD

John Calvin: The Man and His Preaching

The Absoluteness of God

John Calvin would approve beginning this chapter with God and not with himself. Nothing mattered more to Calvin than the supremacy of God over all things. Focus your attention, then, on God's self-identification in Exodus 3:14-15. Here we will see the sun in the solar system of John Calvin's thought and life.

God calls Moses and commissions him to go to Egypt and bring his people out of bondage. Moses is frightened at this prospect and raises the objection that he is not the person to do this. God responds by saying, "I will be with you" (Exodus 3:12). Then Moses says, "[When I] say to them, 'The God of your fathers has sent me to you' . . . they may say to me, 'What is His name?' What shall I say to them?" God's response is one of the most important revelations that has ever been given to man:

> And God said to Moses, "I AM WHO I AM"; and He said, "Thus you shall say to the sons of Israel, 'I AM has sent me to you.'" And God, furthermore, said to Moses, "Thus you shall say to the sons of Israel, 'The LORD [יְהוָה], the God of your fathers, the God of Abraham, the God of Isaac, and the God of Jacob, has sent me to you.'

This is My name forever, and this is My memorial-name
to all generations." (Exodus 3:14-15)

In other words, the great, central, biblical name of *Yahweh*
(יְהוָה) is explicitly rooted by God himself in the phrase "I am who
I am" (אֶהְיֶה אֲשֶׁר אֶהְיֶה). "Tell them, *the one who simply and absolutely is* has sent you. Tell them that the essential thing about me
is that I am."

I begin with this biblical self-identification of God because
the unhidden and unashamed aim in this chapter and in this book
is to fan the flame of your passion for the centrality and supremacy
of God. Does not our heart burn when we hear God say, "My
name is, 'I am who I am'"? The absoluteness of God's existence
enthralls the mind—God's never beginning, never ending, never
becoming, never improving, simply and absolutely there to be
dealt with on his terms or not at all.

Let this sink in: God—the God who holds you in being this
moment—never had a beginning. Ponder it. Do you remember the
first time you thought about this as a child or a young teenager?
Let that speechless wonder rise. God never had a beginning! "I
am" has sent me to you. And one who never had a beginning,
but always was and is and will be, defines all things. Whether we
want him to be there or not, he is there. We do not negotiate
what we want for reality. *God* defines reality. When we come
into existence, we stand before a God who made us and owns
us. We have absolutely no choice in this matter. We do not choose
to be. And when we are, we do not choose that God be. No
ranting and raving, no sophisticated doubt or skepticism, has

any effect on the existence of God. He simply and absolutely is. "Tell them 'I am' has sent you."

If we don't like it, we can change, for our joy, or we can resist, to our destruction. But one thing remains absolutely unassailed. God *is*. He was there before we came. He will be there when we are gone. And therefore what matters in ministry above all things is this God. We cannot escape the simple and obvious truth that God must be the main thing in ministry. Ministry has to do with God because life has to do with God, and life has to do with God because all the universe has to do with God, and the universe has to do with God because every atom and every emotion and every soul of every angelic, demonic, and human being belongs to God, who absolutely *is*. He created all that is, he sustains everything in being, he directs the course of all events, because "from Him and through Him and to Him are all things, to Him be the glory forever" (Romans 11:36).

You who are pastors, may God inflame in you a passion for his centrality and supremacy in your ministry, so that the people you love and serve will say, when you are dead and gone, "This man knew God. This man loved God. This man lived for the glory of God. This man showed us God week after week. This man, as the apostle said, was 'filled with all the fullness of God'" (Eph. 3:19).

This is the aim and the burden of this chapter and this book. Not only because it is *im*plicit in the sheer, awesome existence of God, and not only because it is *ex*plicit in the Word of God, but also because David Wells is staggeringly right when he says, "It is this God, majestic and holy in his being . . . who has disappeared from the modern evangelical world."[1] Lesslie Newbigin says much

---

[1] David Wells, *No Place for Truth* (Grand Rapids: Wm. B. Eerdmans Pub. Co., 1993), p. 300.

the same thing. "I suddenly saw that someone could use all the language of evangelical Christianity, and yet the center was fundamentally the self, my need of salvation. And God is auxiliary to that. . . . I also saw that quite a lot of evangelical Christianity can easily slip, can become centered in me and my need of salvation, and not in the glory of God."[2] And, oh, have we slipped. Where are the churches today where the dominant experience is the precious weight of the glory of God?

Calvin's Unremitting Zeal to Illustrate the Glory of God

John Calvin saw the same thing in his own day. In 1538, the Italian Cardinal Sadolet wrote to the leaders of Geneva trying to win them back to the Roman Catholic Church after they had turned to the Reformed teachings. He began his letter with a long conciliatory section on the preciousness of eternal life, before coming to his accusations of the Reformation. Calvin wrote the response to Sadolet in six days in the fall of 1539. It was one of his earliest writings and spread his name as a reformer across Europe. Luther read it and said, "Here is a writing which has hands and feet. I rejoice that God raises up such men."[3]

Calvin's response to Sadolet is important because it uncovers the root of Calvin's quarrel with Rome that would determine his whole life. The issue is not, first, the well-known sticking points of the Reformation: justification, priestly abuses, transubstantiation, prayers to saints and papal authority. All those will come in for discussion. But beneath all of them, the fundamental issue for

---

[2] Quoted in Tim Stafford, "God's Missionary to Us," *Christianity Today*, December 9. 1996, vol. 40, no. 4, p. 29.
[3] Henry F. Henderson, *Calvin in His Letters* (London: J. M. Dent and Co., 1909), p. 68.

John Calvin, from the beginning to the end of his life, was the issue of the centrality and supremacy and majesty of the glory of God. He sees in Sadolet's letter the same thing Newbigin sees in self-saturated Evangelicalism.

Here's what Calvin said to the Cardinal: "[Your] zeal for heavenly life [is] a zeal which keeps a man entirely devoted to himself, and does not, even by one expression, arouse him to *sanctify the name of God*." In other words, even precious truth about eternal life can be so skewed as to displace God as the center and goal. This was Calvin's chief contention with Rome. This comes out in his writings over and over again. He goes on and says to Sadolet that what he should do—and what Calvin aims to do with all his life—is "set before [man], as the prime motive of his existence, *zeal to illustrate the glory of God*."[4]

I think this would be a fitting banner over all of John Calvin's life and work—*zeal to illustrate the glory of God*. The essential meaning of John Calvin's life and preaching is that he recovered and embodied a passion for the absolute reality and majesty of God. That is what I want us to see most clearly. Benjamin Warfield said of Calvin, "No man ever had a profounder sense of God than he."[5] There's the key to Calvin's life and theology.

Geerhardus Vos, the Princeton New Testament scholar, asked the question in 1891, Why has Reformed theology been able to grasp the fullness of Scripture unlike any other branch of Christendom? He answers, "Because Reformed theology took hold of the Scriptures in their deepest root idea. . . . This root

---

[4] John Dillenberger, *John Calvin, Selections from His Writings* (Atlanta: Scholars Press, 1975), p. 89 (emphasis added).

[5] Benjamin Warfield, *Calvin and Augustine* (Philadelphia: The Presbyterian and Reformed Publishing Co., 1971), p. 24.

idea which served as the key to unlock the rich treasuries of the Scriptures was *the preeminence of God's glory in the consideration of all that has been created*."[6] It's this relentless orientation on the glory of God that gives coherence to John Calvin's life and to the Reformed tradition that followed. Vos said that the "all-embracing slogan of the Reformed faith is this: the work of grace in the sinner is a *mirror for the glory of God*."[7] Mirroring the glory of God is the meaning of John Calvin's life and ministry.

When Calvin did eventually get to the issue of justification in his response to Sadolet, he said, "You . . . touch upon justification by faith, the first and keenest subject of controversy between us. . . . Wherever the knowledge of it is taken away, *the glory of Christ is extinguished*."[8] So here again we can see what is fundamental. Justification by faith is crucial. But there is a deeper reason why it is crucial. The glory of Christ is at stake. Wherever the knowledge of justification is taken away, the glory of Christ is extinguished. This is always the deepest issue for Calvin. What truth and what behavior will "illustrate the glory of God"?

For Calvin, the need for the Reformation was fundamentally this: Rome had "destroyed the glory of Christ in many ways — by calling upon the saints to intercede, when Jesus Christ is the one mediator between God and man; by adoring the Blessed Virgin, when Christ alone shall be adored; by offering a continual sacrifice in the Mass, when the sacrifice of Christ upon the Cross is complete and sufficient,"[9] by elevating tradition to the

---

[6] Geerhardus Vos, "The Doctrine of the Covenant in Reformed Theology," in *Redemptive History and Biblical Interpretation: The Shorter Writings of Geerhardus Vos* (Phillipsburg, NJ: Presbyterian and Reformed Publishing Co., 1980), pp. 241-242 (emphasis added).

[7] Vos, "The Doctrine of the Covenant in Reformed Theology," p. 248 (emphasis added).

[8] Dillenberger, *John Calvin, Selections from His Writings*, p. 95 (emphasis added).

[9] T. H. L. Parker, *Portrait of Calvin* (Philadelphia: Westminster Press, 1954), p. 109.

level of Scripture and even making the word of Christ dependent for its authority on the word of man.[10] Calvin asks, in his *Commentary on Colossians*, "How comes it that we are 'carried about with so many strange doctrines' (Hebrews 13:9)?" And he answers, "Because the excellence of Christ is not perceived by us."[11] In other words, the great guardian of biblical orthodoxy throughout the centuries is a passion for the glory and the excellency of God in Christ. Where the center shifts from God, everything begins to shift everywhere. Which does not bode well for doctrinal faithfulness in our own non-God-centered day.

Therefore the unifying root of all of Calvin's labors is his passion to display the glory of God in Christ. When he was thirty years old, he described an imaginary scene of himself at the end of his life, giving an account to God, and said, "The thing [O God] at which I chiefly aimed, and for which I most diligently labored, was, that the glory of thy goodness and justice . . . might shine forth conspicuous, that the virtue and blessings of thy Christ . . . might be fully displayed."[12]

Twenty-four years later, unchanged in his passions and goals, and one month before he actually did give an account to Christ in heaven (he died at age fifty-four), he said in his last will and testament, "I have written nothing out of hatred to any one, but I have always faithfully propounded what I esteemed to be *for the glory of God.*"[13]

---

[10] John Calvin, *Institutes of the Christian Religion*, I, vii, 1. "A most pernicious error widely prevails that Scripture has only so much weight as is conceded to it by the consent of the church. As if the eternal and inviolable truth of God depended upon the decision of men!"

[11] Parker, *Portrait of Calvin*, p. 55.

[12] Dillenberger, *John Calvin, Selections from His Writings*, p. 110.

[13] Ibid., p. 42 (emphasis added).

The Origin of Calvin's Passion for the Supremacy of God

What happened to John Calvin to make him a man so mastered by the majesty of God? And what kind of ministry did this produce in his life?

He was born July 10, 1509, in Noyon, France, when Martin Luther was twenty-five years old and had just begun to teach the Bible in Wittenberg. We know almost nothing of his early home life. When he was fourteen, his father sent him to study theology at the University of Paris, which at that time was untouched by the Reformation and steeped in Medieval theology. But five years later (when Calvin was nineteen) his father ran afoul of the church and told his son to leave theology and study law, which he did for the next three years at Orleans and Bourges.

During these years Calvin mastered Greek and was immersed in the thought of Duns Scotus and William Occam and Gabriel Biel, and he completed his law course. His father died in May of 1531, when Calvin was twenty-one. Calvin felt free then to turn from law to his first love, which had become the classics. He published his first book, a *Commentary on Seneca*, in 1532, at the age of twenty-three. But sometime during these years he was coming into contact with the message and the spirit of the Reformation, and by 1533 something dramatic had happened in his life.

In November 1533, Nicholas Cop, a friend of Calvin, preached at the opening of the winter term at the University of Paris and was called to account by the Parliament for his Lutheran-like doctrines. He fled the city, and a general persecution broke out against what King Francis I called "the cursed Lutheran sect." Calvin was among those who escaped. The connection with

Cop was so close that some suspect Calvin actually wrote the message that Cop delivered. So by 1533 Calvin had crossed the line. He was now wholly devoted to Christ and to the cause of the Reformation.

What had happened? Calvin recounts, seven years later, how his conversion came about. He describes how he had been struggling to live out the Catholic faith with zeal . . .

> . . .when, lo, a very different form of doctrine started up, not one which led us away from the Christian profession, but one which brought it back to its fountain . . . to its original purity. Offended by the novelty, I lent an unwilling ear, and at first, I confess, strenuously and passionately resisted . . . to confess that I had all my life long been in ignorance and error. . . .
>
> I at length perceived, as if light had broken in upon me [a very key phrase, in view of what we will see], in what a sty of error I had wallowed, and how much pollution and impurity I had thereby contracted. Being exceedingly alarmed at the misery into which I had fallen . . . as in duty bound, [I] made it my first business to betake myself to thy way [O God], condemning my past life, not without groans and tears.[14]
>
> God, by a sudden conversion subdued and brought my mind to a teachable frame. . . . Having thus received some taste and knowledge of true godliness, I was immediately inflamed with [an] intense desire to make progress.[15]

What was the foundation of Calvin's faith that yielded a life devoted utterly to displaying the glory and majesty of God? The answer seems to be that Calvin suddenly, as he says, saw and

---

[14] Ibid., pp. 114-115.
[15] Ibid., p. 26.

tasted in Scripture the majesty of God. And in that moment, both God and the Word of God were so powerfully and unquestionably authenticated to his soul that he became the loving servant of God and his Word the rest of his life. This experience and conviction dethroned the Church as the authority that accredits the Scriptures for the saints. The majesty of God himself in the Word was sufficient for this work.[16]

How this happened is extremely important, and we need to see how Calvin himself describes it in the *Institutes*, especially Book I, Chapters VII and VIII. Here he wrestles with how we can come to a saving knowledge of God through the Scriptures. His answer is the famous phrase, "the internal testimony of the Holy Spirit." For example, he says, "Scripture will ultimately suffice for a saving knowledge of God only when its certainty is founded upon the inward persuasion of the Holy Spirit" (I, viii, 13). So two things came together for Calvin to give him a "saving knowledge of God"—Scripture and the "inward persuasion of the Holy Spirit." Neither alone suffices to save.

But how does this actually work? What does the Spirit do? The answer is not that the Spirit gives us added revelation to what is in Scripture[17] but that he awakens us, as from the dead,

---

[16] Calvin, as he so often did, laid hold on Augustine to strengthen his claim that this was the historic position of the Church, in spite of the Roman Catholic teaching that the Church authorizes the Scriptures for the believer. Commenting on Augustine's view of the role of the authority of the church in leading to a well-founded faith in Scripture, Calvin wrote in the *Institutes*, "He only meant to indicate what we also confess as true: those who have not yet been illumined by the Spirit of God are rendered teachable by reverence for the church, so that they may persevere in learning faith in Christ from the gospel. Thus, he avers, the authority of the church is an introduction through which we are prepared for faith in the gospel. For, as we see, he wants the certainty of the godly to rest upon a far different foundation" (I, vii, 3).

[17] J. I. Packer, "Calvin the Theologian," in James Atkinson, et al., editors, *John Calvin: A Collection of Essays* (Grand Rapids: Wm. B. Eerdmans Publishing Co., 1966), p. 166. "Rejecting both the Roman contention that the Scripture is to be received as authoritative on the church's authority, and with it the idea that Scripture could be proved divinely authoritative by rational argument alone, Calvin affirms Scripture to be self-authenticating through the inner witness of the Holy Spirit. What is this 'inner witness'? Not a special quality of experience, nor a new, private revelation, nor an existential 'decision,' but a work of enlightenment."

to see and taste the divine reality of God in Scripture, which authenticates it as God's own Word. He says, "Our Heavenly Father, revealing his majesty [in Scripture], lifts reverence for Scripture beyond the realm of controversy" (I, viii, 13). There is the key for Calvin: The witness of God to Scripture is the immediate, unassailable, life-giving revelation to our minds of *the majesty of God* that is manifest in the Scriptures themselves. The "majesty of God" is the ground of our confidence in his Word.

Over and over again in his description of what happens in coming to faith you see his references to the majesty of God revealed in Scripture and vindicating Scripture. So already in the dynamics of his conversion the central passion of his life is being ignited.

We are almost at the bottom of this experience now. If we go just a bit deeper we will see more clearly why this conversion resulted in such an "invincible constancy" in Calvin's lifelong allegiance to the majesty of God and the truth of God's Word. Here are the words that will take us deeper.

> Therefore illumined by [the Spirit's] power, we believe neither by our own [note this!] nor by anyone else's judgment that Scripture is from God; but above human judgment we affirm with utter certainty (just as if we were gazing upon the majesty of God himself) that it has flowed to us from the very mouth of God by the ministry of men.[18]

This is almost baffling. He says that his conviction concerning the majesty of God in Scripture rests not on any human judg-

---

[18] *Institutes*, I, vii, 5.

ment, not even his own. What does he mean? Perhaps the words of the apostle John shed the most helpful light on what Calvin is trying to explain. Here are the key words from 1 John 5:7-11:

> And it is the Spirit who bears witness, because the Spirit is the truth. . . . If we receive the witness of men, the witness of God [= the Spirit] is greater; for the witness of God is this, that He has borne witness concerning His Son. . . . And the witness is this, that God has given us eternal life, and this life is in His Son.

In other words, the "witness of God," that is, the inward witness of the Spirit, is greater than any human witness—including, John would probably say in this context, the witness of our own judgment. And what is that witness of God? It is not merely a word delivered to our judgment for reflection, for then our conviction would rely on that reflection. What is it then? Verse 11 is the key: "The witness is this: that God has given us eternal life." I take that to mean that God witnesses to us of his reality and the reality of his Son and his Word by giving us life from the dead so that we come alive. His witness is the gift of spiritual life. His witness is that we come alive to his majesty and see him for who he is in his Word. In that instant we do not reason from premises to conclusions—we see that we are awake, and there is not even a prior human judgment about it to lean on. When Lazarus was awakened in the tomb by the call or the "witness" of Christ, he knew without reasoning that he was alive and that this call had wakened him.

Here's the way J. I. Packer puts it:

The internal witness of the Spirit in John Calvin is a work of enlightenment whereby, through the medium of verbal testimony, the blind eyes of the spirit are opened, and divine realities come to be recognized and embraced for what they are. This recognition, Calvin says, is as immediate and unanalyzable as the perceiving of a color, or a taste, by physical sense—an event about which no more can be said than that when appropriate stimuli were present it happened, and when it happened we knew it had happened.[19]

So in his early twenties John Calvin experienced the miracle of having the blind eyes of his spirit opened by the Spirit of God. And what he saw immediately, and without any intervening chain of human reasoning, were two things, so interwoven that they would determine the rest of his life: the majesty of God and the Word of God. The Word mediated the majesty, and the majesty vindicated the Word. Henceforth he would be a man utterly devoted to displaying the majesty of God by the exposition of the Word of God.

The Ministry Made by the Divine Majesty of the Word

What form would that ministry take? Calvin knew what he wanted. He wanted the enjoyment of literary ease so he could promote the Reformed faith as a literary scholar.[20] That is what he thought he was cut out for by nature. But God had radically different plans—as he had for Augustine and Luther—and for many of us who did not plan our lives the way they have turned out.

After escaping from Paris and finally leaving France entirely, Calvin spent his exile in Basel, Switzerland, between 1534 and

---

[19] Packer, "Calvin the Theologian," p. 166.
[20] Dillenberger, *John Calvin, Selections from His Writings*, p. 86.

1536. To redeem the time, "he devoted himself to the study of Hebrew."[21] (Imagine such a thing! Would any pastor today, exiled from his church and country, and living in mortal danger, study Hebrew? What has become of the vision of ministry that such a thing seems unthinkable today?) In March of 1536, he published in Basel the first edition of his most famous work, *The Institutes of the Christian Religion*, which would go through five enlargements before reaching its present form in 1559. And we should not think that this was a merely academic exercise for Calvin. Years later he tells us what was driving him:

> But lo! while I lay hidden at Basel, and known only to few people, many faithful and holy persons were burnt alive in France. . . . It appeared to me, that unless I opposed [the perpetrators] to the utmost of my ability, my silence could not be vindicated from the charge of cowardice and treachery. This was the consideration which induced me to publish my *Institutes of the Christian Religion*. . . . It was published with no other design than that men might know what was the faith held by those whom I saw basely and wickedly defamed.[22]

So when you hold the *Institutes* of John Calvin in your hand, remember that theology, for John Calvin, was forged in the furnace of burning flesh, and that Calvin could not sit idly by without some effort to vindicate the faithful and the God for whom they suffered. I think we would, perhaps, do our theology better today if more were at stake in what we said.

In 1536, France gave a temporary amnesty to those who had

---

[21] Theodore Beza, *The Life of John Calvin* (Milwaukee, OR: Back Home Industries, 1996, from 1844 Edinburgh edition of the Calvin Translation Society), p. 21.

[22] Dillenberger, *John Calvin, Selections from His Writings*, p. 27.

fled. Calvin returned, put his things in order, and left, never to return, taking his brother Antoine and sister Marie with him. He intended to go to Strasbourg and continue his life of peaceful literary production. But he wrote later to a friend, "I have learned from experience that we cannot see very far before us. When I promised myself an easy, tranquil life, what I least expected was at hand."[23] A war between Charles V and Francis I resulted in troop movements that blocked the road to Strasbourg, and Calvin had to detour through Geneva. In retrospect, one has to marvel at the providence of God that he should so arrange armies to position his pastors where he wanted them.

The night that he stayed in Geneva, William Farel, the fiery leader of the Reformation in that city, found out he was there and sought him out. It was a meeting that changed the course of history, not just for Geneva, but for the world. Calvin tells us what happened in his preface to his commentary on Psalms:

> Farel, who burned with an extraordinary zeal to advance the gospel, immediately learned that my heart was set upon devoting myself to private studies, for which I wished to keep myself free from other pursuits, and finding that he gained nothing by entreaties, he proceeded to utter an imprecation that God would curse my retirement, and the tranquillity of the studies which I sought, if I should withdraw and refuse to give assistance, when the necessity was so urgent. By this imprecation I was so stricken with terror, that I desisted from the journey which I had undertaken.[24]

The course of his life was irrevocably changed. Not just geo-

---

[23] Parker, *Portrait of Calvin*, p. 24.
[24] Dillenberger, *John Calvin, Selections from His Writings*, p. 28.

graphically, but vocationally. Never again would Calvin work in what he called the "tranquillity of . . . studies." From now on, every page of the forty-eight volumes of books and tracts and sermons and commentaries and letters that he wrote would be hammered out on the anvil of pastoral responsibility.

He took up his responsibilities in Geneva first as Professor of Sacred Scripture, and within four months was appointed Pastor of St. Peter's church—one of the three parishes in the 10,000-person town of Geneva. But the City Council was not altogether happy with Farel or Calvin because they did not bow to all their wishes. So the two of them were banished in April 1538.

Calvin breathed a sigh of relief and thought God was relieving him from the crush of pastoral duties so he could be about his studies. But when Martin Bucer found out about Calvin's availability, he did the same thing to get him to Strasbourg that Farel had done to get him to Geneva. Calvin wrote, "That most excellent servant of Christ, Martin Bucer, employing a similar kind of remonstrance and protestation as that to which Farel had recourse, before, drew me back to a new station. Alarmed by the example of Jonah which he set before me, I still continued in the work of teaching."[25] That is, he agreed to go to Strasbourg and teach. In fact, for three years Calvin served as the pastor to about 500 French refugees in Strasbourg, as well as teaching New Testament. He also wrote his first commentary, on Romans, and put out the second enlarged edition of the *Institutes*.

Perhaps the most important providence during this three-year stay in Strasbourg was finding a wife. Several had tried to get Calvin a wife. He was thirty-one years old, and numerous

---

[25] Ibid., p. 29.

women had shown interest. Calvin had told his friend and match-maker William Farel what he wanted in a wife: "The only beauty which allures me is this—that she be chaste, not too nice or fastidious, economical, patient, likely to take care of my health."[26] Parker comments, "Romantic love . . . seems to have had no place in his character. Yet prosaic wooing led to a happy marriage."[27] I think Parker was wrong about romantic love (see below on Idelette's death). An Anabaptist widow named Idelette Stordeur was the subject of John Calvin's "prosaic wooing." She and her husband Jean had joined Calvin's congregation. In the spring of 1540, Jean died of plague, and on August 6, 1540, Calvin and Idelette were married. She brought a son and daughter with her into Calvin's home.

Meanwhile back in Geneva, chaos was making the city fathers think that maybe Calvin and Farel were not so bad after all. On May 1, 1541, the City Council rescinded the ban on Calvin and even held him up as a man of God. This was an agonizing decision for Calvin, because he knew that life in Geneva would be full of controversy and danger. Earlier in October he said to Farel that though he preferred not to go, "yet because I know that I am not my own master, I offer my heart as a true sacrifice to the Lord."[28] This became Calvin's motto, and the picture on his emblem included a hand holding out a heart to God with the inscription, *prompte et sincere* ("promptly and sincerely").

On Tuesday, September 13, 1541, he entered Geneva for the second time to serve the church there until his death on May 27,

---

[26] Parker, *Portrait of Calvin*, p. 70.
[27] Ibid., p. 69.
[28] W. de Greef, *The Writings of John Calvin: An Introductory Guide*, trans. Lyle D. Bierma (Grand Rapids: Baker Book House, 1993), p. 38.

1564. His first son, Jacques, was born July 28, 1542, and two weeks later died. He wrote to his friend Viret, "The Lord has certainly inflicted a severe and bitter wound in the death of our baby son. But He is Himself a Father and knows best what is good for his children."[29] This is the kind of submission to the sovereign hand of God that Calvin rendered in all of his countless trials.

Idelette was never well again. They had two more children who also died at or soon after birth. Then on March 29, 1549, Idelette died of what was probably tuberculosis. Calvin wrote to Viret,

> You know well how tender, or rather soft, my mind is. Had not a powerful self-control been given to me, I could not have borne up so long. And truly, mine is no common source of grief. I have been bereaved of the best companion of my life, of one who, had it been so ordained, would have willingly shared not only my poverty but even my death. During her life she was the faithful helper of my ministry. From her I never experienced the slightest hindrance. She was never troublesome to me throughout the whole course of her illness, but was more anxious about her children than about herself. As I feared these private worries might upset her to no purpose, I took occasion three days before she died, to mention that I would not fail in discharging my duty towards her children.[30]

Calvin never remarried. And it is just as well. The pace he kept would not have left much time for wife or children. His acquaintance, Colladon, who lived in Geneva during these years describes his life:

---

[29] Parker, *Portrait of Calvin*, p. 71.
[30] Ibid., *Portrait of Calvin*, p. 71.

Calvin for his part did not spare himself at all, working far beyond what his power and regard for his health could stand. He preached commonly every day for one week in two [and twice on every Sunday, or a total of about ten times every fortnight]. Every week he lectured three times in theology. . . . He was at the *Consistoire* on the appointed day and made all the remonstrances. . . . Every Friday at the Bible Study . . . what he added after the leader had made his *declaration* was almost a lecture. He never failed in visiting the sick, in private warning and counsel, and the rest of the numberless matters arising out of the ordinary exercise of his ministry. But besides these ordinary tasks, he had great care for believers in France, both in teaching them and exhorting and counseling them and consoling them by letters when they were being persecuted, and also in interceding for them. . . . Yet all that did not prevent him from going on working at his special study and composing many splendid and very useful books.[31]

He was, as Wolfgang Musculus called him, "a bow always strung." In one way he tried to take heed to his health, but probably did more harm than good. Colladon says that "he took little regard to his health, mostly being content for many years with a single meal a day and never taking anything between two meals. . . ." His reasons were that the weakness of his stomach and his migraines could only be controlled, he had found by experiment, by continual abstinence.[32] But on the other hand, he was apparently careless of his health and worked night and day with scarcely a break. You can hear the drivenness in this letter to Falais

---

[31] T. H. L. Parker, *Calvin's Preaching* (Louisville: Westminster/John Knox Press, 1992), pp. 62-63.
[32] Quoted in T. H. L. Parker, *John Calvin, A Biography* (Philadelphia: Westminster Press, 1975), p. 104.

in 1546: "Apart from the sermons and the lectures, there is a month gone by in which I have scarce done anything, in such wise I am almost ashamed to live thus useless."[33] A mere twenty sermons and twelve lectures in that month!

To get a clearer picture of his iron constancy, add to this work schedule the continuous ill health he endured. He wrote to his physicians in 1564 when he was fifty-three years old and described his colic and spitting of blood and ague and gout and the "excruciating sufferings" of his hemorrhoids.[34] But worst of all seemed to be the kidney stones that had to pass, unrelieved by any sedative.

> [They] gave me exquisite pain. . . . At length not without the most painful strainings I ejected a calculus which in some degree mitigated my sufferings, but such was its size that it lacerated the urinary canal and a copious discharge of blood followed. This hemorrhage could only be arrested by an injection of milk through a syringe.[35]

On top of all this pressure and physical suffering were the threats to his own life. "He was not unfamiliar with the sound of mobs outside his house [in Geneva] threatening to throw him in the river and firing their muskets."[36] On his deathbed, Calvin said to the pastors gathered, "I have lived here amid continual bickerings. I have been from derision saluted of an evening before my door with forty or fifty shots of an arquebus [a large gun]."[37] In a letter to Melanchthon in 1558, he wrote that war was imminent

---

[33] Ibid., pp. 103-104.
[34] Dillenberger, *John Calvin, Selections from His Writings*, p. 78.
[35] Ibid., p. 78.
[36] Parker, *Portrait of Calvin*, p. 29.
[37] Dillenberger, *John Calvin, Selections from His Writings*, p. 42.

in the region and that enemy troops could reach Geneva within half an hour. "Whence you may conclude," he said, "that we have not only exile to fear, but that all the most cruel varieties of death are impending over us, for in the cause of religion they will set no bounds to their barbarity."[38] In other words, he went to sleep, when he slept, pondering from time to time what sorts of tortures would be inflicted on him if the armies entered Geneva.

One of the most persistent thorns in Calvin's side were the libertines in Geneva. But here too his perseverance was triumphant in a remarkable way. In every city in Europe men kept mistresses. When Calvin began his ministry in Geneva in 1536 at the age of twenty-seven, there was a law that said a man could keep only one mistress.[39] After Calvin had been preaching as pastor in St. Peter's church for over fifteen years, immorality was still a plague, even in the church. The libertines boasted in their license. For them the "communion of saints" meant the common possession of goods, houses, *bodies, and wives.* So they practiced adultery and indulged in sexual promiscuity in the name of Christian freedom. And at the same time they claimed the right to sit at the Lord's Table.[40]

The crisis of the Communion came to a head in 1553. A well-to-do libertine named Berthelier was forbidden by the Consistory of the church to eat the Lord's Supper but appealed the decision to the Council of the City, which overturned the ruling. This created a crisis for Calvin who would not think of yielding to the state the rights of excommunication, nor of admitting a libertine to the Lord's Table.

---

[38] Ibid., p. 71.
[39] Parker, *Portrait of Calvin,* p. 29.
[40] Henderson, *Calvin in His Letters,* p. 75.

The issue, as always, was the glory of Christ. He wrote to Viret, "I . . . took an oath that I had resolved rather to meet death than profane so shamefully the Holy Supper of the Lord. . . . My ministry is abandoned if I suffer the authority of the Consistory to be trampled upon, and extend the Supper of Christ to open scoffers. . . . I should rather die a hundred times than subject Christ to such foul mockery."[41]

The Lord's day of testing arrived. The libertines were present to eat the Lord's Supper. It was a critical moment for the Reformed faith in Geneva.

> The sermon had been preached, the prayers had been offered, and Calvin descended from the pulpit to take his place beside the elements at the communion table. The bread and wine were duly consecrated by him, and he was now ready to distribute them to the communicants. Then on a sudden a rush was begun by the troublers in Israel in the direction of the communion table. . . . Calvin flung his arms around the sacramental vessels as if to protect them from sacrilege, while his voice rang through the building: "These hands you may crush, these arms you may lop off, my life you may take, my blood is yours, you may shed it; but you shall never force me to give holy things to the profaned, and dishonor the table of my God."

> "After this," says Beza, Calvin's first biographer, "the sacred ordinance was celebrated with a profound silence, and under solemn awe in all present, as if the Deity Himself had been visible among them."[42]

The point of mentioning all these woes in Geneva is to set in

---

[41] Ibid., p. 77.
[42] Ibid., pp. 78-79.

bold relief the invincible constancy of John Calvin in the ministry that God had called him to. We asked earlier, What happened to John Calvin to make him a man so mastered by the majesty of God? And what kind of ministry did this produce in his life? We answered the first question by saying that Calvin experienced the supernatural inward witness of the Spirit to the majesty of God in Scripture. Henceforth, everything in his thinking and writing and ministry was aimed at illustrating the majesty and glory of God.

Now what is the answer to the second question—what kind of ministry did his commitment to the majesty of God produce? Part of the answer has been given: It produced a ministry of incredible steadfastness—a ministry, to use Calvin's own description of faithful ministers of the Word, of "invincible constancy."[43] But that is only half the answer. It was a ministry of unrelenting exposition of the Word of God. The constancy had a focus, the exposition of the Word of God.

Calvin had seen the majesty of God in the Scriptures. This persuaded him that the Scriptures were the very Word of God. He said, "We owe to the Scripture the same reverence which we owe to God, because it has proceeded from Him alone, and has nothing of man mixed with it."[44] His own experience had taught him that "the highest proof of Scripture derives in general from the fact that God in person speaks in it."[45] These truths led to an inevitable conclusion for Calvin. Since the Scriptures are the very voice of God, and since they are therefore self-authenticating in revealing

---

[43] In a sermon on Job 33:1-7, Calvin calls preachers to constancy: "When men so forget themselves that they cannot subject themselves to Him Who has created and fashioned them, it behooves us to have an *invincible constancy*, and to reckon that we shall have enmity and displeasure when we do our duty; yet nevertheless let us go through it without bending." John Calvin, *Sermons from Job by John Calvin* (Grand Rapids: Wm. B. Eerdmans Publishing Co., 1952), p. 245.

[44] Quoted in Packer, "Calvin the Theologian," p. 162.

[45] *Institutes*, I, vii, 4.

the majesty of God, and since the majesty and glory of God are the reason for all existence, it follows that Calvin's life would be marked by "invincible constancy" in the exposition of Scripture.

He wrote tracts, he wrote the great *Institutes*, he wrote commentaries (on all the New Testament books except Revelation, plus the Pentateuch, Psalms, Isaiah, Jeremiah, and Joshua), he gave biblical lectures (many of which were published as virtual commentaries), and he preached ten sermons every two weeks. But *all* of it was exposition of Scripture. Dillenberger said, "[Calvin] assumed that his whole theological labor was the exposition of Scripture."[46] In his last will and testament he said, "I have endeavored, both in my sermons and also in my writings and commentaries, to preach the Word purely and chastely, and faithfully to interpret His sacred Scriptures."[47]

Everything was exposition of Scripture. This was the ministry unleashed by seeing the majesty of God in Scripture. The Scriptures were absolutely central because they were absolutely the Word of God and had as their self-authenticating theme the majesty and glory of God. But out of all these labors of exposition, preaching was supreme. Emile Doumergue, the foremost biographer of John Calvin with his six-volume life of Calvin, said, as he stood in the pulpit of John Calvin on the 400th anniversary of Calvin's birth, "That is the Calvin who seems to me to be the real and authentic Calvin, the one who explains all the others: Calvin the preacher of Geneva, molding by his words the spirit of the Reformed of the sixteenth century."[48]

Calvin's preaching was of one kind from beginning to end:

---

[46] Dillenberger, *John Calvin, Selections from His Writings*, p. 14.
[47] Ibid., p. 35ff.
[48] Quoted by Harold Dekker, "Introduction," *Sermons from Job by John Calvin*, p. xii.

He preached steadily through book after book of the Bible. He never wavered from this approach to preaching for almost twenty-five years of ministry in St. Peter's church of Geneva—with the exception of a few high festivals and special occasions. "On Sunday he took always the New Testament, except for a few Psalms on Sunday afternoons. During the week . . . it was always the Old Testament."[49] The records show fewer than half a dozen exceptions for the sake of the Christian year. He almost entirely ignored Christmas and Easter in the selection of his text.[50]

To give you some idea of the scope of Calvin's pulpit, he began his series on the book of Acts on August 25, 1549, and ended it in March 1554. After Acts he went on to the epistles to the Thessalonians (forty-six sermons), Corinthians (186 sermons), the pastoral epistles (eighty-six sermons), Galatians (forty-three sermons), Ephesians (forty-eight sermons)—until May 1558. Then there is a gap when he was ill. In the spring of 1559, he began the Harmony of the Gospels and was not finished when he died in May 1564. On the weekdays during that season he preached 159 sermons on Job, 200 on Deuteronomy, 353 on Isaiah, 123 on Genesis, and so on.[51]

One of the clearest illustrations that this was a self-conscious choice on Calvin's part was the fact that on Easter Day, 1538, after preaching, he left the pulpit of St. Peter's, banished by the City Council. He returned in September 1541—over three years later—and picked up the exposition in the next verse.[52]

---

[49] Parker, *Portrait of Calvin*, p. 82.

[50] John Calvin, *The Deity of Christ and Other Sermons*, trans. Leroy Nixon (Grand Rapids: Wm. B. Eerdmans Pub. Co., 1950), p. 8.

[51] For these statistics see Parker, *Portrait of Calvin*, p. 83, and W. de Greef, *The Writings of John Calvin: An Introductory Guide*, pp. 111-112.

[52] Parker, *Calvin's Preaching*, p. 60.

Why this remarkable commitment to the centrality of sequential expository preaching? Three reasons are just as valid today as they were in the sixteenth century.

First, Calvin believed that the Word of God was a lamp that had been taken away from the churches. He said in his own personal testimony, "Thy word, which ought to have shone on all thy people like a lamp, was taken away, or at least suppressed as to us. . . . And now, O Lord, what remains to a wretch like me, but . . . earnestly to supplicate thee not to judge according to [my] deserts that fearful abandonment of thy word from which, in thy wondrous goodness thou hast at last delivered me."[53] Calvin reckoned that the continuous exposition of books of the Bible was the best way to overcome the "fearful abandonment of [God's] Word."

Second, Parker says that Calvin had a horror of those who preached their own ideas in the pulpit. He said, "When we enter the pulpit, it is not so that we may bring our own dreams and fancies with us."[54] He believed that by expounding the Scriptures as a whole, he would be forced to deal with all that *God* wanted to say, not just what *he* might want to say.

Third—and this brings us full circle to the beginning, where Calvin saw the majesty of God in his Word—he believed with all his heart that the Word of God was indeed the Word of *God*, and that all of it was inspired and profitable and radiant with the light of the glory of God. In Sermon number 61 on Deuteronomy he challenged pastors of his day and ours:

Let the pastors boldly dare all things *by the word of God.*
. . . Let them constrain all the power, glory, and excel-

---

[53] Dillenberger, *John Calvin, Selections from His Writings*, p. 115.
[54] Parker, *Portrait of Calvin*, p. 83.

lence of the world to give place to and to obey *the divine majesty of this word.* Let them enjoin everyone by it, from the highest to the lowest. Let them edify the body of Christ. Let them devastate Satan's reign. Let them pasture the sheep, kill the wolves, instruct and exhort the rebellious. Let them bind and loose thunder and lightning, if necessary, *but let them do all according to the word of God.*[55]

The key phrase here is "the divine majesty of this word." This was always the root issue for Calvin. How might he best show forth for all of Geneva and all of Europe and all of history the majesty of God? He answered with a life of continuous expository preaching. There would be no better way to manifest the full range of the glories of God and the majesty of his being than to spread out the full range of God's Word in the context of the pastoral ministry of shepherding care.

This is why preaching remains a central event in the life of the church even 500 years after the printing press and the arrival of radio and TV and cassettes and CDs and computers. God's Word is mainly about the majesty of God and the glory of God. That is the main issue in ministry. And even though the glory and majesty of God in his Word can be known in the still, small voice of whispered counsel by the bedside of a dying saint, there is something in it that cries out for expository exultation. This is why preaching will never die. And radical, pervasive God-centeredness will always create a hunger for preaching in God's people. If God is "I am who I am"—the great, absolute, sovereign, mysterious, all-glorious God of majesty whom Calvin saw in

---

[55] John Calvin, *Sermons on the Epistle to the Ephesians* (Edinburgh: Banner of Truth, 1973), p. xii (emphasis added).

Scripture, there will always be preaching, because the more this God is known and the more this God is central, the more we will feel that he must not just be analyzed and explained, he must be acclaimed and heralded and magnified with expository exultation. The flaming legacy of Sovereign Joy, lit so bright in the life of Augustine, and spread through centuries of fervent saints, is ignited anew in every generation by glowing, God-besotted preaching—the preaching of the "divine majesty of this word." May God grant every preacher of the Word such a "taste" of Sovereign Joy in God and such an "intense desire" for him that expository exultation would flame up in every church.

CONCLUSION

Four Lessons from the Lives of Flawed Saints

The swans are not silent. And this is a great mercy. We may feel like crickets chirping in the presence of St. Augustine, or tiny echoes of Luther and Calvin. But our sense of inadequacy only magnifies the grace of hearing their voices and seeing their lives so long after they have lived. They were not perfect, which makes them the more helpful in our battle to be useful in spite of frailty. I thank God for the privilege of knowing these famous, flawed saints.

The lessons from their stories for our lives are rich with hope, no matter how humbling. Of many more that could be distilled and savored, I close with four.

1. *Do not be paralyzed by your weaknesses and flaws.*

Oh, how many times we are tempted to lick our wounded pride and shrink from some good work because of the wounds of criticism—especially when the criticism is true! A sense of being weak and flawed can paralyze the will and take away all passion for a worthy cause. Comparison with others can be a crippling occupation. When it comes to heroes, there is an easy downward slip from the desire for imitation to the discouragement of intimidation to the deadness of resignation. But the mark of humility and faith and maturity is to stand against the paralyzing effect of famous saints. The triumphs they achieved over their own flagrant sins and flaws should teach us not to be daunted by our own.

God never yet used a flawless man, save one. Nor will he ever, until Jesus comes again.

In the case of our weaknesses, we must learn with the apostle, and the swans who sang his Song after him, that the grace of Christ is sufficient, and that his strength is made perfect in weakness. We must learn from the Scripture and from the history of weak victors to say, "Most gladly, therefore, I will rather boast about my weaknesses, that the power of Christ may dwell in me" (2 Corinthians 12:9). The suffering of weak saints can make them sink with defeat or make them strong. From Paul, Augustine, Luther, and Calvin, we can learn to say, "I take pleasure in infirmities, in reproaches, in necessities, in persecutions, in distresses for Christ's sake: for when I am weak, then am I strong" (2 Corinthians 12:10, KJV).

In the case of our flaws and our sins, we must learn gutsy guilt. This is what we see, especially in Luther. The doctrine of justification by faith alone did not make him indifferent to practical godliness, but it did make him bold in grace when he stumbled. And well it should, as Micah 7:8-9 declares: "Do not rejoice over me, O my enemy. Though I fall I will rise; though I dwell in darkness, the LORD is a light for me. I will bear the indignation of the LORD because I have sinned against Him, until He pleads my case and executes justice for me. He will bring me out to the light, and I will see His righteousness."

Even when we have "sinned against him"—even when we "bear the indignation of the LORD"—we say to the accusing and gloating adversary, "Do not rejoice over me. . . . Though I fall I will rise." The Lord himself, who frowns in chastisement, will be my irresistible advocate and he will triumph in court for me. He will plead my case. He will be my light. The cloud will pass. And I will stand in righteousness, not my own, and do the work he has given me to do.

Oh, let us learn the secret of gutsy guilt from the steadfastness of sinful saints who were not paralyzed by their imperfections. God has a great work for everyone to do. Do it with all your might—yes, and even with all your flaws and all your sins. And in the obedience of this faith, magnify the glory of his grace, and do not grow weary in doing good.

2. In the battle against sin and surrender, learn the secret of sovereign joy.

Few have seen this or modeled it for us like Augustine. The quest for holiness is the quest for satisfaction in God. And satisfaction in God is a divine gift of sovereign joy. It is sovereign because, in its fullness, it triumphs over all contestants for the heart. The duration of Augustine's bondage only serves to make the power of his deliverance more compelling. It was the bondage of "fruitless joys" that could only be driven out by a superior—a sovereign—pleasure.

> How sweet all at once it was for me to be rid of *those fruitless joys* which I had once feared to lose! . . . *You drove them from me*, you who are the true, the *sovereign joy*. You drove them from me and took their place, you who are *sweeter than all pleasure*. . . . O Lord my God, my Light, my Wealth, and my Salvation.[1]

No one taught more powerfully than Augustine that the heart is made for God, and that nothing else will drive out the suitors of sin but the happiness of knowing our true Husband. "You made us for yourself, and our hearts find no peace till they rest in you."[2]

---

[1] Aurelius Augustine, *Confessions*, p. 181 (IX, 1), emphasis added.
[2] Ibid., p. 21 (I, 1).

Many have said with Augustine that "he is happy who possesses God."[3] But not as many have seen and said that this happiness is a sovereign delight that sanctifies the soul with idol-evicting jealousy. This is what we must learn. The battle to be holy—the battle for sanctification—is a battle fought at the level of what we love, what we cherish and treasure and delight in.

To be sure there is real self-denial and real discipline and gouging out of the eye and cutting off of the hand—a spiritual severity of warfare that many have not attained. But it must be said—and let the apostle say it with all authority—that the secret beneath this severe discipline, the secret to severing all else as rubbish, is to savor Christ as gain (Philippians 3:8).

The battle for holiness is a battle to be fought mainly by fueling the fires of our passion for Christ. Sanctification is the triumph of "sovereign joy." Its legacy is a legacy of love.

3. *Supernatural change comes from seeing Christ in his sacred Word.*

The sanctifying power of sovereign joy does not arise in a blind soul. "*Beholding* the glory of the Lord, [we] are being changed into his likeness from one degree of glory to another" (2 Corinthians 3:18, RSV, emphasis added). But where do we "behold" this glory of the Lord? The New Testament answers: in "the light of the *gospel* of the glory of Christ, who is the image of God . . . [that is, in] the light of the *knowledge* of the glory of God in the face of Christ" (2 Corinthians 4:4, 6, emphasis added).

Notice the words "knowledge" and "gospel." We see the glory of Christ in the "gospel." We see the glory of God through "knowl-

---

[3] Thomas A. Hand, *Augustine on Prayer* (New York: Catholic Book Publishing Co., 1986), p. 17 (*On the Happy Life*, 11).

edge." The glory of the Lord, whom to see truly is "sovereign joy," is seen in a gospel, a knowledge, a message, a Word. Oh, how Luther drove this truth with relentless force against fanatics with their added revelations and against Catholics with their added traditions.

We must learn from Luther that the Word became flesh, and the Word became Greek sentences. We behold the glory of the incarnate Word through the grammar of the written Word. Sacred study is a way of seeing, especially when combined with prayer. *Oratio* and *meditatio*—prayer and meditation—were the pathway to supernatural sight of the glory of God in the face of Christ.

Oratio: "Incline my heart to thy testimonies, and not to gain!" (Psalm 119:36, RSV). "Open my eyes, that I may behold wondrous things out of thy law" (Psalm 119:18, RSV). "[I pray] that the God of our Lord Jesus Christ, the Father of glory, may give to you a spirit of wisdom and of revelation in the knowledge of Him . . . that the eyes of your heart may be enlightened" (Ephesians 1:17-18). This was not just any prayer, but prayer over the Word and prayer to love the Word and prayer for light from the Word.

Meditatio: "His delight is in the law of the LORD, and in His law he meditates day and night. And he will be like a tree firmly planted by streams of water, which yields its fruit in its season, and its leaf does not wither; and in whatever he does, he prospers" (Psalm 1:2-3). "Faith comes by hearing and hearing by the word of Christ" (Romans 10:17). "Sanctify them in the truth; your word is truth" (John 17:17). After years of pounding on the Greek text of the apostle Paul, it finally yielded, and Luther saw the glory of Christ in the Gospel and entered into paradise. His life and labor bear witness to this crucial truth: The sight of Christ that wakens sovereign joy is mediated through the written word. Even though flesh and blood does not reveal the glory of the Son, neither is it revealed apart from the ordinary work of hearing and meditating on the Word of God (Matthew 16:17; Romans 10:17).

We are sanctified in the truth because the truth (revealed and written) displays the glory of Christ, which begets the sovereign joy, which severs the root of sin and sets us free.

4. *Therefore, let us exult over the exposition of the truth of the Gospel and herald the glory of Christ for the joy of all peoples.*

When John Calvin saw the majesty of God in his Word, he was taken captive to preaching. Preaching, for John Calvin, was the faithful, regular exposition of the Word of God with a passion for the glory of Christ. It was exposition, but it was also exultation. Exultation over the majesty of God and the glory of Christ revealed in the written Word produced expository exultation. That is what I call preaching. Calvin's devotion to preaching through all his life, as one of the greatest theologians who ever lived, is a trumpet call for all of us—laypeople and preachers—to exult over the exposition of the Word.

Let churches ring with expository exultation! Let laypeople love the hearing of this great God-saturated sound! Let seminaries breed the passions of Calvin, Luther, and Augustine for the majesty of God that takes the soul captive and binds it to the Word, which reveals Christ and wakens sovereign joy. If a worshiping heart and a holy life are the fruit of sovereign joy, and if the written Word of God is the deposit of historical truth where the glory of Christ wakens this joy, then let us pray that God would raise up generations of preachers who give themselves, with Calvin-like devotion, to expository exultation over the glory of Jesus Christ for the joy of all peoples.

A NOTE ON RESOURCES
DESIRING GOD MINISTRIES

If you would like to ponder further the vision of God and life presented in this book, we at Desiring God Ministries (DGM) would love to help you. DGM is a resource ministry of Bethlehem Baptist Church in Minneapolis, Minnesota. Our desire is to fan the flame of your passion for God and help you spread that passion to others. We have hundreds of resources available for this purpose. Most of our inventory consists of books and audiotapes by John Piper. In addition, we produce God-centered children's curricula and we host conferences and coordinate John Piper's conference speaking schedule.

Since money is not our treasure we try to keep our prices as low as possible. And since we don't want money to be a hindrance to the gospel, if our prices are more than you can pay at this time, our *whatever-you-can-afford* policy applies to almost all of our resources—even if you can't afford to pay anything! This policy is intended for individuals and we request that folks limit these orders to 3-4 items at a time. We also accept VISA, MasterCard and Discover credit cards for convenience and speed, but we would rather give you resources than have you go into debt.

DGM exists to help you make God your treasure. Because God is most glorified in you when you are most satisfied in him.

For more information or to request a free resource catalog, call us or visit our web site.

1-888-346-4700 toll free in the USA
(612) 373-0651 international calls
(612) 338-4372 fax
www.desiringGOD.org
mail@desiringGOD.org

DESIRING GOD MINISTRIES
720 Thirteenth Avenue South
Minneapolis, Minnesota, 55415-1793

(612) 338-7653 Bethlehem Baptist Church

INDEX OF SCRIPTURES

INDEX OF PERSONS

INDEX OF SUBJECTS